# Mastering
# Trading
# Stress

Founded in 1807, John Wiley & Sons is the oldest independent publishing company in the United States. With offices in North America, Europe, Australia and Asia, Wiley is globally committed to developing and marketing print and electronic products and services for our customers' professional and personal knowledge and understanding.

The Wiley Trading series features books by traders who have survived the market's ever changing temperament and have prospered—some by reinventing systems, others by getting back to basics. Whether a novice trader, professional or somewhere in-between, these books will provide the advice and strategies needed to prosper today and well into the future.

For a list of available titles, visit our Web site at www.WileyFinance.com.

# Mastering Trading Stress

## Strategies for Maximizing Performance

**ARI KIEV**

John Wiley & Sons, Inc.

Published by John Wiley & Sons, Inc., Hoboken, New Jersey.
Published simultaneously in Canada.

Wiley Bicentennial Logo: Richard J. Pacifico.

For general information on our other products and services or for technical support, please contact our Customer Care Department within the United States at (800) 762-2974, outside the United States at (317) 572-3993 or fax (317) 572-4002.

Wiley also publishes its books in a variety of electronic formats. Some content that appears in print may not be available in electronic formats. For more information about Wiley products, visit our Web site at www.wiley.com.

***Library of Congress Cataloging-in-Publication Data:***

Kiev, Ari.
  Mastering trading stress : strategies for maximizing performance / Ari Kiev.
    p. cm. — (Wiley trading series)
  Includes index.
  ISBN 978-0-470-18168-3 (cloth)
 1. Investments—Psychological aspects.   2. Speculation—Psychological aspects.
3. Hedge funds.  I. Title.
  HG4515.15.K54 2008
  332.601′9—dc22

                                                         2007020337

10  9  8  7  6  5  4  3  2  1

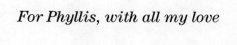

*For Phyllis, with all my love*

# Contents

# Preface

Success in trading, as in other high-performance tasks, requires the ability to master your fears and other emotional and behavioral responses to stress so that you can develop workable processes for profitable results in the face of the uncertainty, change, and complexity of the markets. This means learning to manage the stress of the markets, drawdowns, and the challenges associated with commitment to outsized results by stretching oneself and entering the zone of discomfort, which is a prelude to extraordinary performance.

There are any number of paradigms that can be followed in understanding stress. Given the increasing awareness of the concept of post-traumatic stress disorder (PTSD), which describes a specific anxiety syndrome associated with exposure to life-threatening events, I have decided to rely on aspects of that paradigm to explore some of the experiences associated with the traumatic psychological effects encountered with major drawdowns while managing a portfolio of stocks.

The loss of money often sets in motion a progressive development of such symptoms as psychological numbing, distress, paralysis, and confusion that are seen in PTSD, which therefore provides a useful framework for understanding the impact of financial disaster on those who work as traders or portfolio managers. Moreover, many of the behavioral patterns of avoidance, withdrawal, and risk aversion, and even sometimes specific deep-value approaches to long-term investing, often develop as a result of an earlier traumatic experience in losing money.

Most of the traders I write about have worked in hedge funds, a psychologically taxing environment because of the focus on absolute returns. Unlike banks or mutual funds, the hedge fund requires you to work on yourself to produce successful results. This in itself creates stress and requires different kinds of adjustments to the work process than you might encounter in a long-only longer-term horizon at a mutual fund. This kind of intense environment creates considerable stress, which must be mastered in some way by the trader and portfolio manager in order to produce outperformance. This requires a fair amount of self-examination so as to learn to ride out the emotional swings associated with market volatility and profit-and-loss (P&L) volatility.

The most successful traders have developed processes that enable them to set and reach their goals. A critical aspect of this process is to master stress not only in terms of their portfolio management processes, but also by building teamwork and leadership skills, as well as learning to ride out their own emotional responsivity to the fluctuations associated with the markets.

Because portfolio managers are ultimately the instrument of their own success, it is important that they learn to read their emotional and psychological signals as well as those of others in the game. The purpose of this book is to help elucidate some of the dimensions of stress, how it is experienced, and how it interferes with the trading process and to learn some techniques and principles for dealing with it, so as to enhance performance.

As in my previous books, I have relied heavily on actual case studies and dialogues with traders to help underscore and frame their experiences. The value of hearing of the experiences of others is that you learn that you are not alone and that you, too, can master your own distress by learning to face the issues openly. As in my previous books, I have disguised the names of companies because I have been more interested in focusing on trading strategies and ways of overcoming the stress of trading, especially in market downturns, short squeezes, or drawdowns, which are particularly problematic situations for traders. I have also disguised the identities of traders to protect their privacy and to focus on the generic principles to be extracted from their experiences.

ARI KIEV

# Acknowledgments

M any people have helped me with this book. I am especially grateful to the hedge fund managers who have provided me with the opportunity to explore the interface between trading and psychology. I am indebted to the many traders who shared their personal experiences with me as well as those who read and commented on the manuscript in its earlier form. I want to thank Grace Lichtenstein for helping me to organize an enormous amount of interview material and for her efforts in editing several versions of the original manuscript. Tricia Brown was especially helpful in fine-tuning subsequent drafts and preparing the book for publication. As in the past, much of this would not have been done without the support of my beloved wife Phyllis, who has always been there to encourage me.

A.K.

# Introduction

You don't need to know the difference between amaranth, the high-altitude grain, and Amaranth, the failed company, to know that the hedge fund world has become a turbulent one.

As the size, holdings, and sheer number of hedge funds have proliferated worldwide in the past few years, the stress felt by traders in the hedge fund world has multiplied. The industry has become far more competitive, the regulatory environment more assertive, the shadow of "Dr. Drawdown" more ominous. In 1990, only a handful of hedge funds existed, managing just $39 billion. By 2006 there were some 9,000 hedge funds managing $1.3 trillion.* The crowded marketplace is far more hectic than it once was.

The ups and downs have become steeper and scarier because of the weak results that some hedge funds have registered in recent times. Returns have declined at some funds, while even giants, such as Amaranth Advisors, have failed. More than ever, traders must pay close attention day in and day out. This only increases the need to manage stress and keep it from interfering with a trader's focus.

The daily grind of the trader has always been full of excitement, full of energy, full of adventure, full of stress. One minute the room might be quiet while everyone intensely watches a stock. The next minute a national terror alert may be issued, and everything seems to go temporarily insane in the markets. And a trader's thoughts are as diverse as his workplace. In one instant, he is comparing his numbers to those of the trader sitting next to him or worrying that the risk manager is headed his way. The next minute he may be thinking about problems at home or pondering whether he will make enough money to buy the bigger house his family needs.

While many traders live for the thrill of trading, most also feel the emotional, psychological, and physical impact of the constant changes. Imagine riding a roller coaster for eight hours a day, five days a week, 48 weeks out of the year. Even the most avid thrill seeker could grow weary. More than anything else, the specter of rampant drawdowns has become the

---

*"Hedging on Hedge Funds," editorial, *New York Times*, November 30, 2006.

quintessential source of stress, leading some funds to heavy redemptions and forcing some companies to close individual funds. When that happens, very few recover. I view the stress of drawdowns as severe enough to cause emotional reactions that can mimic post-traumatic stress disorder.

This book is my fifth in a series for traders about building and maintaining the emotional stamina to perform at peak levels. It is both a sequel to my most recent previous title, *Hedge Fund Masters* (2005), and the first to view stress from the perspective of the current challenging and changing trading atmosphere at hedge funds. I have written it to help both those who are new to my books as well as those who have read one or more of them.

New research continues to validate that stress is not only psychologically debilitating, but also physically damaging. And the results of stress are magnified by each experience. In other words, your past experiences with stress intensify your reactivity to future stresses. Stress literally changes who we are. As we deal with more and varied degrees of stress, our bodies become more acutely sensitive to stress. Thus, less stressful events can trigger increasingly greater stress responses. For example, our bodies when exposed to something like unusually high traffic when we are running late for an important meeting can (and often do) react as if we are experiencing a life-threatening event.

This isn't just something mental. The stress response is a combination of chemical reactions in the brain and body that produce physical and emotional symptoms—including sweaty palms, a racing heart, and blurred vision. Stress is now also being linked to many common ailments such as ulcers, headaches, and fatigue. In fact, a constancy of this type of biochemical reaction may even lead to other more serious disorders such as cancer, strokes, and heart disease.

You may think this is an exaggeration, but it is not. Consider that each time your body is under stress, there is a release of chemicals and hormones that are intended to give you the extra nudge you would need to respond to a threat. When you become increasingly exposed to stress, then there are more of these chemicals and hormones being released. What happens as a result is still being studied, but it appears that some of the chemicals may begin to chip away at your immune system. Some of the hormones eat at your digestive tract or lungs. Some of the chemicals constrict blood vessels and raise blood pressure, and high levels of other chemicals may even kill off brain cells. By studying the various effects of these reactions, researchers are beginning to link stress to a wide variety of ailments ranging from obesity and osteoporosis to baldness and memory loss.

While stress is in large part simply an unavoidable aspect of life, these sobering facts should weigh heavily on those whose professions are by nature innately stressful. And although traders have not cornered the market on stress, their jobs are certainly high on the list. Of course, some traders just seem naturally better equipped to deal with the emotional turmoil of trading. Others seem to fall apart under much less dire circumstances. This may be a result of personality, family history, genetics, attitude, or a combination of all of these. What is more important than determining why people experience stress in varying degrees is discovering what can be done to reduce the stress response—especially in those who are more likely to overreact to stressful situations.

One thing is for certain: There is no quick fix. And telling someone to "buck up" and "get over it" doesn't help, either. So, what's a trader to do?

While eliminating stress is neither realistic nor an entirely desired approach, *reducing* stress is. Traders can perhaps best cope with stress by being proactive and taking steps to reduce the stressfulness of their careers. In this book, I discuss various ways of doing this—beginning with developing an appropriate understanding of stress and how it physically affects us and leading all the way to the implementation of specific exercises that can help traders manage their daily stress.

Because there is no standard answer for every person, a large part of this book includes examples, transcripts of conversations, and personality profiles with other traders. I hope that you will be able to relate to the experiences that these traders are working through. Because stress often leads to carelessness, which leads to failure and therefore more stress, these examples offer insight into how stress directly impacts the trading decisions you make. They also provide various ways of dealing with or reducing the stress in an effort to trade more effectively. It is my hope that you will directly relate to some of the individuals described throughout this book and will literally be able to learn from their mistakes. In addition, I describe a variety of stress-reducing techniques that you can use. By trying several different techniques, you should be able to generate your own approach to stress management.

There is no way to take the stress out of trading, and if you did you would probably also remove many of the very elements that make this profession so exciting and enticing. But stress does not have to make you emotionally, mentally, or physically ill, and it does not have to hinder your trading game. You can learn to reduce your stress, cope with the stresses that are inevitable, and even use stress to your own benefit. In the pages that follow, you can learn important coping mechanisms, which, I hope, will make your work as a trader even more rewarding.

# Mastering Trading Stress

# CHAPTER 1

# The Nature of Stress

## What Is Stress and Why Is It a Problem?

**W**alter was a 28-year-old bond trader who was working a block away from the World Trade Center when disaster struck in 2001. His office building was successfully evacuated. Yet when the financial markets resumed operations, he struggled to return to the winning ways he had enjoyed in his relatively short career up to that time. He attributed the downturn in his performance mostly to the downturn in the economy but felt his excitement about his work diminishing.

Then one afternoon, about a year after 9/11, his heart began thumping wildly and he suffered chest pains. Fearing a heart attack, associates called an ambulance, and Walter was rushed to a hospital where cardiologists performed tests for hours before concluding that the episode was nothing more than a case of stress and acid reflux. Walter took small comfort in this. For weeks, he felt tightness in his chest every time he took a big position in the market. He lost all interest in his profession and went into what he thought was a profound depression. He left his job and believed that his life was spiraling downward.

In outlining his troubles, Walter convinced me that before 9/11 he had enjoyed a healthy appetite for the risks and stress that financial work entailed. He had taken some positions that proved unwise but had accepted them in stride. I sensed that the "heart attack" incident was a major symptom of the anxiety that had gripped him in the wake of the terrorist attack. Then all of a sudden it appeared: Walter could no longer tolerate risk. When I suggested this to him, he argued heatedly at first that he had not changed but was simply going through a "bad patch."

*Sometime later, however, Walter read an article about a survey show-ing how hundreds of people in the downtown New York financial com-munity were exhibiting similar feelings. As we started to talk, his voice began to quaver and tears streaked down his cheeks. "It's true!" he said. "I could be one of the people in this survey. I've felt out of control since the moment the markets reopened after 9/11." As Walter calmed down, he began opening up about all the anxious moments he had endured for so many months. The first phase of his recuperation was under way.*

Stress. We all experience it. We hardly need a definition for it. Everyone knows what stress is, because everyone has been exposed to some form of it. Even children, who don't necessarily know the name for it, have felt its symptoms—knots in the stomach, nausea, a throbbing headache, a racing heart, sweaty palms, knocking knees.

If stress is unavoidable in everyday life, it is even more so in the hectic, fast-paced world of trading—where millions and millions of dollars are on the line with every decision. Therefore, it is imperative that traders learn how to deal with stress. Notice I said "deal with," not "eliminate."

In fact, when you learn to understand the bodily sensations related to stress, you can also discover how to step outside yourself and begin to learn how to control those sensations. The problem is less *what* you are feeling than *how* you are interpreting these feelings and reacting to them. Anger, anxiety, and excitement differ from each other only in the *inter-pretation* of the physical experience—how you choose to handle that ex-perience. Recognizing the automatic response to real or imagined danger, you will be able to experience your feelings in a more hopeful way without reacting to them as if something were wrong.

## THE FIGHT-OR-FLIGHT ALARM

The body's response to stress is meant to be adaptive, helping you to cope with dangerous situations. It prepares you for fight—stand your ground—or flight—flee the situation—by increasing blood flow to the mus-cles, increasing heart rate and breathing rate, emptying the stomach and gastrointestinal tract of blood, and heightening your senses.

When you become anxious or fearful, your body's physiological reac-tion is to pump adrenaline into the bloodstream. This is your body's nat-ural or automatic response to danger, novel stimuli, or symbolic risks. Your heart rate increases, and you may experience palpitations. Your breathing will speed up, and it may be difficult to catch your breath. You may start huffing and puffing as if you had exerted yourself. Dizziness, lightheadedness, difficulty swallowing, and butterflies in your stomach are also common accompaniments of the adrenaline response.

While Walter, the trader profiled at the beginning of this chapter, experienced a truly life-threatening trauma on 9/11, these same symptoms often burst forth in the fast-paced world of trading. They might be a response to the stresses of business or to memories of past trading experiences, not to actual danger. Regardless, your body reacts the same. It becomes overloaded. Your capacity to cope effectively is significantly reduced by the overreaction of your nervous system. You expend excess energy to reduce these reactions or to hide or control them. And if you don't recognize that this is happening and don't attempt to deal with these responses, you are likely to become overwhelmed.

Of course, it is natural to want to be in control. So, you react by trying to hide or reject these feelings or, in another control attempt, you may tighten or tense up your body even more. But it doesn't work. The adrenaline keeps on pumping. As you deny your responses instead of owning them or letting them pass, your stress level tends to increase rather than decrease. Your anxiety escalates. Rather than recognize and heed your body's signals by slowing down, resting, relaxing, and regrouping so that you can accurately assess and handle the reality before you, you are caught between the escalation of symptoms that you cannot deny and your need to stay in control.

The more panicky you feel, the less willing you are to let go and allow yourself to experience the feelings. Under this increasing amount of stress, it becomes impossible or near impossible for you to relax and to allow the waves of adrenaline to course naturally through your body. Rather than going with the flow, you are likely to identify the anxiety with the origin of the stress and then assiduously learn to avoid that activity or awakening that memory. Then, your anxiety-reducing rituals or compulsions become even more debilitating than the original anxiety.

This happens especially when someone has been losing money and is in negative profit and loss (P&L) territory. The tendency for some is to blame the risk manager or management rather than face up to the difficulties that they have been having with their trading. So denial of responsibility and projection of blame onto others sometimes shows up in this context.

Let me use the real-life experience of a trader named Stuart. He has been frustrated because he doesn't think there is a good fit between his trading style—a long-term company-specific, intensive, fundamentals-driven approach to investment—and the shorter-term model that his firm prefers. He is particularly upset because he has to deal on a regular basis with a risk manager who he believes doesn't understand financial investment. He also feels that the risk manager doesn't appreciate how well he has done and that he has complied with the drawdown limits of his contract by staying fixed at 5 percent down.

As you will see in the discussion that follows, this trader has started to understand that his feelings are no more than an alarm reaction coupled with an interpretation of danger and a fear of losing control. The same applies to you if you are in a similar situation. Once you can see that there is a sequence of responses to events, you can observe events *without* reacting to them. Only then will you begin to isolate your interpretation from the event itself.

## Case Study: Stress and Panic Reaction

In this dialogue, the trader describes how the fight-or-flight response has led him to make spur-of-the-moment decisions out of reactivity. He has learned that by organizing a plan, documenting his experiences, and taking a few moments before decision making, he can help overcome the stressful symptoms that often lead to panic and bad decisions.

**Stuart:**  Stress leads you to do more work and to make sure that your ideas are that much stronger. I think this is definitely a high-stress job.

**Kiev:**  Sometimes stress is good because it forces you to confront your feelings.

**S:**  It keeps you excited and driven to find that extra data point or to come up with that new idea.

**K:**  What about panic? Have you ever been a situation where you were panicking?

**S:**  There have been situations where stocks have blown up and we are long or short, and it goes against us. Your first reaction can sometimes be the wrong one. Sometimes you need to sit back and say, "If the stock is opening up at five dollars, maybe everyone is feeling the same way that we are." They are scared that they are short and all of a sudden there is good news and the stock is being lifted up. You may want to sit back and say, "Let's not do anything until we figure out what the numbers are. Let's talk to the companies." Is it really justified that the stock is down 15 percent, or should it be down only 7 percent? You may want to wait it out and try to evaluate it from there.

**K:**  Sometimes the panic is worse.

**S:**  Sometimes you can't decide what to do. Then it's a frenzy, and you get out, and all of a sudden the stock has come down and it goes back to flat on the day.

**K:**  Over time, have you have learned to ride out these emotions?

S:         You learn to deal with the stress and the anxiety. One of the prob-
           lems that I had when I first got here was just a lack of experience.
           There would be a terror alert, and the market would start selling
           off. We would be like "Oh, there is a terror alert!" We would start
           shorting, and then all of a sudden we'd learn that the terror alert
           was false. The stocks came ripping back and we were left won-
           dering what to do: "Do I cover the shorts that I just put on?" I
           went from shorting them on the fear to feeling "Okay, when ev-
           eryone is panicking, buy the dip." Over time you become more
           comfortable. Now I have a plan, and I deal with the situations
           instead of panicking.
K:         Is panic the worst kind of psychological experience?
S:         Absolutely! You feel like you have no control in that situation.

## DIFFERENCES IN STRESS RESPONSES

While all traders experience the kinds of stress that you do, it is also important to note that not everyone reacts to stress in the same way. Although the fight-or-flight process is biologically the same, not everyone
experiences the *same* symptoms or the same *intensity* of stress-related
symptoms.

Consider the following stock analysts whom I recently spoke to. Sey-
mour was frustrated about what he described as the "condescending" attitude of Michael, the senior analyst, toward him. He felt Michael was more
concerned about being right than just making money. I suggested that he
look more closely at himself and his own attitude and see what he could do
to improve his performance and contribute the most that he could without
taking Michael's criticism personally. In particular, I suggested that he talk
to Michael about improving communication and trying to raise the level of
the game. He could establish a set of criteria with Michael so that he could
provide more of what Michael was looking for. Thus they would both move
toward being on the same page and create a better team approach.

Meanwhile, another analyst, Gilbert, was becoming anxious about being responsible for close to $500 million of positions. He decided to cut
back and reduce his level of anxiety. I agreed that this was a good strategy.
My suggestion was that he stretch, and when the stretch becomes too uncomfortable, pull back and preserve capital. Then do the work and build
up the positions again.

A different trader, Tad, was going through a bad patch. He was down
about $4 million for the year; $6 million is his "down and out" (the amount
of loss that triggers the shutting down of a portfolio). As he debated
whether to start trading again, I suggested that if he could, he should start

small when he has a high-conviction idea, and that he pay close attention to the risk/reward and stop-out levels of the trades. I also suggested he monitor some of his emotional responses and psychological concerns by keeping a diary. He had done this a year earlier and got a lot of benefit from it.

Tad was a member of Dave's team. He was having some problems dealing with Dave's emotionality when things weren't going well for him. When I spoke to him about this, I found out that Dave was very much like Tad's own father, suggesting a reason why Tad has been drawn to Dave. In psychological terms, Tad reexperiences something familiar in both the good sense and the bad sense. He re-creates some of his earlier psychological experiences by way of trying to master his response to them. On some level this is working, and he is getting some greater awareness about his own predilections.

These situations raise a number of questions: Are some people more prone to develop stress-related symptoms? Are there any personality characteristics that make it harder for some people to cope with stress? Can stress be completely avoided? If not, can you learn how to tolerate stress more effectively? Can stress be beneficial to any degree?

Many psychological disorders involving stress have been proven to have biological underpinnings. So, there are biological components connected to the way in which you handle stress. However, while anyone can experience stress and there are no specific personality traits that predispose people to it, there do seem to be certain personality characteristics that make it especially difficult to let go of the symptoms of stress once they develop. A trader may not have all of these characteristics, but it is useful to understand them as additional variables that may make it difficult to handle stress. They mark you as a prime candidate for anxiety, and contribute to the way in which you handle stress.

Let me offer an analogy that those of you who are parents have probably observed or that apply to your own childhood. Some babies are calm and even unresponsive to noise or environmental stimuli. They sleep through loud music, fire engines, or ambulances and seem unflappable. Other babies seem predisposed to anxiety. They are hyperalert and respond to the slightest stirring in their environment. From birth they may seem hyperactive and fine-tuned to the most subtle nuances of reaction in their parents and siblings. This sensitivity often continues throughout the rest of their lives. The positive side is that extreme sensitivity is often expressed in artistic perception in later life. The negative side is a tendency to overreact to environmental stimuli such that you become excessively alert to the stimuli around you and prone to react to them. A person who has been more sensitive to stimuli, therefore, would understandably have a harder time dealing with stress, especially extremely stressful situations.

While everyone is exposed to some form of stress in their lifetimes, if you have been traumatized as a child you may have already developed a set of defensive reactions that can influence the way you respond to stress. These defense mechanisms may make you more vulnerable to the development of certain symptoms.

As a result of chaos in the home, whether in the form of physical abuse, sexual molestation, conflict, suppression, or ridicule, you may have learned an adaptive style or social persona designed to protect you from stress. At the same time, your creative self may have been suppressed or stifled. You may have withdrawn from reality such that you are not flexible or able to learn from your past experiences. Perhaps you are out of touch with your true or hidden potential and thus not able to be fulfilled in the course of your trading career. Your sense of self-esteem may be low, and you may function in the world with a sense that you must keep hiding your secret self. You may feel a sense of guilt, inadequacy, and shame, which you try to mask with your efforts to perform better.

An additional experience of childhood, which may make for greater sensitivity to stress or at least put you at greater risk for the kinds of symptoms experienced with stress, is a fear of abandonment. If you were neglected, rejected, or abandoned as a child, or even if you were left alone for what seemed to you to be an extraordinary amount of time, you may be extra sensitive to stressful events, which in turn disturb your sense of stability and universal order. When such events occur, they may spark the underlying fear of abandonment and dissolution of self. For traders, who work with very random and unpredictable markets, the lack of anchoring here can be especially disconcerting.

In part, what makes stressful events so traumatic is that they have the force of igniting these primordial fears of childhood. Exposed to a stressful event, you are overwhelmed by a massive emotional and physiological emergency. Such a reaction is like a flash flood that temporarily swamps your psyche and renders all of your prior adaptive skills inoperable. Your belief systems become ineffective for coping, and you feel as if you are drowning in the fear and panic associated with a sense of impending doom. Following the initial shock, you become intensely sensitized to subsequent events and are then likely to engage in a variety of defensive maneuvers designed to reduce the intensity of the pain. These patterns may become self-perpetuating and may keep the fear alive.

## PERSONALITY FACTORS

A predilection for control and perfectionism increases the chances that you will have difficulty handling stress, particularly when you discover that you cannot control the sources of it. This was the case with Albert, a very bright analyst who had difficulty not being in control of the many facets of the job in which he was engaged. After being a bit stressed out for several weeks, Albert made a conscious effort to stay focused, to spend fewer nights out on the town, and to take some time off and prepare for the end of the year. It paid off for him and he was pleased, overall, with his performance.

## THE STAGES OF STRESS

While I have described the fundamental nature of stress, I want to underscore the fact that stress develops in stages. For some traders, one stage may represent a more daunting struggle than the others. It is, therefore, important to understand the stages and what specific problems may arise within each.

### Initial Stage

The initial stage includes symptoms of anxiety, depression, shock, and confusion. Some people stay locked in this initial stage, and their symptoms may persist long after the stressful event. They may never progress to the subsequent phases, or they may experience them briefly and then revert back to the original anxiety syndrome. When the initial shock responses persist, they may begin to complain of depressive symptoms or exhibit tachycardia (rapid cardiac pulse), hyperventilation, or a dysfunctional bowel or bladder. They become regular visitors to medical clinics with complaints of physical illness.

### Secondary Stage

At other times, stress may lead to behavioral patterns: memory loss, hypervigilance (always on alert or with narrowed attention, and constantly checking and rechecking one's environment), inability to concentrate, emotional distancing, emotional numbing, and a tendency to deny the reality of the event. When these symptoms persist as the dominant feature of stress, the trader is likely to complain of a sense of emptiness, feelings of vulnerability, and a sense of depersonalization. He may complain that nothing seems real and that he feels like a robot. Emotionally numbed, he becomes unable to read the responses of others and feels extremely suspicious, distrustful, and doubtful.

This secondary stage also has earmarks of an obsessive-compulsive disorder with recurrent, uncontrolled intrusive thoughts, emotional detachment, still more suspicion, and loss of identity. As one person described it: "I don't know who I am. I cannot be certain if I am who I think I am, and I certainly can't trust other people. It's as if I am disconnected from my feelings and can't trust my instincts. So, I don't know how to read situations. I sometimes think other people are working through me, or that I am merely the vehicle for another force."

A case in point along these lines was Jamie, who lost a lot of money in 2004 and was not able to come out of the negative downward spiral. In October 2006 he was very negative about the markets and the possibility that the midterm elections the following month might not be decisive and might trigger a lot of recounts and litigation. He was shorting the dollar and the market but very cautiously, because he had no cushion. Jamie was looking for bigger opportunities but would approach them with greater awareness of risk management principles.

Earlier in the year, Jamie had been up about $15 million. He had hoped to get to $50 million, but because of a few bad bets he lost the $15 million. He was bummed out and became very risk-averse because he didn't want to lose more. Jamie felt that he would be up for the year if he had stayed with fixed income trades and not switched to currencies and commodities. He didn't really trade with a specific target in mind or with the idea of sizing his bets based on his conviction level. He was more dependent on momentum moves, which hadn't happened for him or in his space.

## Third Stage

The third stage of stress is characterized by the persistence of intrusive thoughts about the stressful event during sleeping and waking hours. This includes unresolved and persistent problems with guilt, fear, anger, and grief. Traders may keep replaying past trades in a neurotic or compulsive way such that they experience each trade as if it were being repeated. This serves only to set in motion a self-fulfilling prophecy of doubt, shame, suspicion, avoidance, withholding, and the persistence of negative emotions. When a trader reacts to the negative symptoms and emotions of stress this way, he is likely to continue to see no new opportunities. He will repeatedly feel rejected or humiliated and feel pressure to respond to new trades in the same self-protective patterns—if he decides to trade at all. Thus, the cycle continues. This will most certainly lead to a lack of satisfaction and fulfillment and an inability to meet career goals or visions.

This was the case with Tad, who was trying to get back his groove. Since the middle of 2003 when he was up $6 million, he hadn't been able to sustain his streak, and lost his trust in his instinct to get into a trade and especially to get out of a trade when it wasn't working. He became too attached to his longer-term analytical ideas and did not pay as much attention to the markets. Since Tad was part of a larger portfolio, his portfolio manager decided to stop his trading until he could find some ideas. Tad would rather trade small, even in his personal account, with the hope of recapturing the feeling so that he could rely on his instinct when the opportunity presented itself.

## Stage Four

The trader who is experiencing third-stage types of symptoms may naturally feel helpless and hopeless. If this state continues, it can lead to a fourth and even more serious stage of stress characterized by chronic depression and a variety of other syndromes, including becoming accident prone or exhibiting daredevil behavior designed to produce a temporary alleviation of distress. Some victims may enter into high-adrenaline-producing activities in order to create an extraordinary sense of omnipotence that numbs their sense of inadequacy and thwarts the emotional pain of memory. Generally, however, such activities and the highs associated with them are short-lived, and the individual soon finds himself again depressed—empty and drained of vitality. Then the victim may seek relief in alcohol, drugs, or other substances, thus initiating a new problem.

## TAKING IT STEP-BY-STEP

Most likely you have not considered the possibility that you can learn to live with and even use your stress rather than mask it. You may not have considered that your own sense of powerlessness and victimization has created much of the way you experience the world.

Walter, the trader who was profiled at the beginning of the chapter, was one person who successfully navigated this transition. After he acknowledged how his anxiety had overtaken him following the terrorist attack on 9/11, he could start rebuilding his career, bit by bit. He didn't jump in and start trading big positions the day after his breakthrough, of course. He waded, rather than dove, back into the roiling waters of the stock market, beginning with small trades. Along with more therapy and medication, he learned the relaxation exercise I discuss in Chapter 14, and performed it each morning before plunging into his workday. Gradually, he was able to once again accept the normal anxiety that is part of his profession.

And you can, too. Stress does not have to result in a self-cycling pattern of negativity. A first step is to look at how much you are trying to change the circumstances around you rather than accepting them as they are. Aristotle wrote that "a thing is a thing," and yet we tend to project our own interpretations onto situations far more than is justifiable. Indeed, the true task of this book is to assist you in learning to accept things as they are and to stop attributing more meaning to them than they deserve. It is critical to distinguish between events and your interpretations of them. I will return to this concept again in later chapters; for now, try to accept this as a key to managing your stress. Each new situation is full of possibility if you can only approach it in that way.

## KEY SYMPTOMS OF STRESS

- Shortness of breath
- Dizziness
- Faintness
- Numbness
- Tingling in the extremities
- Palpitations
- Gagging
- Choking
- Esophageal and gastric reflux
- Butterflies in the stomach
- Diarrhea
- Urinary urgency and frequency
- Nausea
- Blurred vision
- Confusing thoughts
- Inability to concentrate

# CHAPTER 2

# The Emotions of Stress

## What Negative Emotions Are Experienced as a Result of Stress?

*T*odd was anticipating a capitulation and was long bonds. All the signals suggested that things in the equity market were getting worse and that his long bond trade was working. He made $1 million and felt really good. Then he was caught in a rally and gave a lot of his profits back. He spiraled into a state of panic and despair—convinced that he was no good as a trader. He failed to take his trade off in the stock market rally, and his P&L dropped from being up 23 percent for the year to being up only 15 percent.

In retrospect, after reviewing his trading, Todd realized that he should have taken off a good part of his profits when he had them and reduced the size of his risk at the moment he saw the equity markets turning upward. Instead he allowed his emotions to color the way in which he traded.

Navigating the emotions of the trading world can feel like being a running back zigzagging forward and back to elude tacklers on a football field. Ranging from fear to frustration, elation to anger, you can experience all the ups and downs in a day's work. And whether you want to admit it or not, your emotions do affect your financial decisions—leading to insecurity, anxiousness, disappointment, failure, negativity, and even withdrawal.

As one trader noted, "Trading sets in motion a whole different set of behavioral and emotional responses that are quite different from the need for perfect information and models." Therefore, the more you can understand the emotions of trading and how they affect your trading decisions, the better trader you will become.

In this chapter, I outline a few of the emotions that may surge through you as a result of stress. In the next chapter, I discuss in more detail the dangers of stress and how stress leads to trading errors; and finally, in the fourth chapter, I suggest some of the ways that you can counteract these negative emotions.

## FEAR AND GREED

Two emotions that play an important part in your trading career are fear and greed. Some pundits have noted that greed dominates a bull market, and fear dominates a bear market. Not only can you experience both emotions during any given trading day, but you can even experience them in response to the same trade.

How can you know whether fear and excessive ambition are influencing your trading decisions? If you are excessively ambitious, you may begin to feel a false sense of bravado about your wins, set unrealistic expectations of annual growth, start making riskier investments, rely on less secure sources of information, jump on someone else's bandwagon more often, and justify losses without considering mistakes.

For example, Dean was up about $2.5 million and got hungry for huge gains. Thinking he could double his money, he wound up losing the entire bet. Reviewing what went wrong, it turns out that he was trying to hit a home run, when in fact he should have been taking some profits off the table since he had been flat on the year until this month. Palmer is another trader who has had a problem with the need for big gains. He was feeling discouraged about losing $6 million for the month when he was stuck in a short squeeze and didn't take his profit soon enough. More intensive inquiry, however, revealed that while Palmer had been right on his call initially, he then developed a taste for outsized gains, trying to take a shot because he felt he had a cushion. This was the third time he had been in a major drawdown because of the impulse to get bigger without doing the commensurate work, which is often the key factor. In the future he is going to try to be bigger earlier in the move and to recognize his natural inclination to get bigger at the wrong time.

Whereas greed can be characterized as a desire to jump in too quickly, fear elicits the opposite response. You may develop a negative attitude and feel powerless and apathetic. Thus you may not recognize the opportunities in front of you, and you may get out of winning trades too quickly.

To counter both of these emotions, it is crucial to follow your investment plan. Recognize that you are feeling this way, but consciously choose to consider your actions in a critical light. Don't follow the crowd when you are feeling like you want to hit a home run with every trade. Don't jump out of trades at the first sign of anxiety. Stick with your plan. Monitor your feelings. And don't let your emotions control your behavior.

Anxiety leads to various patterns, from holding on to losers to getting out of winners too fast.

## Case Study on Holding on to Losers

In this dialogue, Alan talks about how his anxiety manifests itself. In an effort to improve his record, he realizes that he has sometimes made poor choices in size, in timing, or in both.

**Alan:**  Every time I think I have a handle on things, they keep changing. I had higher conviction in smaller-cap names. Then the dynamics of the market changed and they are higher risk. I took a big draw-down and didn't have anything to offset it. I was building up high-conviction ideas and then the world started to work against me. Maybe I should have gotten out sooner. I felt like I was doing the right thing: focusing on a few high-conviction ideas. But all of a sudden it doesn't work.

**Kiev:**  Do you mean you lost confidence?

**A:**  No. It makes you second-guess what you are doing, as opposed to trading around larger, more liquid names. I could have gotten in and out, but that is not where I am going to make incremental dollars over the long term. I had a lot of drawdown in my P&L.

**K:**  If it isn't working, in retrospect should you have gotten out, or you should have taken the pain and bought more when they went down? What is the retrospective view?

**A:**  I still think they are going to work, and I started buying them in the last couple of days. One of the positions started to stabilize and I have a catalyst coming, which I was looking for a few days ago. I'm looking to build up a big position into this catalyst. I need to learn to get biggest in a position to maximize my profitability at the right time, just before the catalyst, as opposed to getting big and then taking the risk over time. That position will work against me and I will build up drawdown and put myself at risk, at the whims of the market.

**K:**  Cut the position as it is going down. Keep enough so as to keep track of it and then prepare to get bigger before the catalyst, when you can get back in at a larger size.

**A:**  I think the catalyst will be three weeks from now. By buying it too soon you put yourself at risk for the three weeks of movement or whatever is going on in the market. In my two biggest drawdowns in terms of high-conviction ideas, nothing changed. I think I got hyped up to get big in a few high-conviction ideas, but timing is everything. If I am critiquing myself, the timing of the positions could go plus or minus.

**K:**     You knew the catalyst was three weeks away and you saw the market wasn't favorable to your stocks? You could have gotten smaller and waited for the catalyst. Or is it so illiquid that you couldn't get in or out?

**A:**     I brought down my exposure by 50 percent. I went from $75 million of exposure to $35 million. How do you perceive what I am doing?

**K:**     What I am hearing you say is that it's portfolio management—trying to find the right ideas as opposed to figuring out where there are opportunities to make money in the next several days. Are you playing for a target number? The sector is a given percentage of the Standard & Poor's (S&P) and therefore ought to account for so much profitability. Positions ought to be sized a certain amount to produce specific profit targets. If you have to make $36 million a year, you have to make $3 million a month or $750,000 a week or $150,000 a day. Are your positions big enough with what you know about catalysts that you can extract that amount each day? Are you thinking where is the money going to be made? Do you have a P&L target? The value of it is to help you design what you are doing in terms of the result.

**A:**     I do think that way—down to the positions that I thought would get me to that goal over a several-week period.

**K:**     What is your target for the year?

**A:**     My target is $1 million a month.

**K:**     That's $50,000 a day. Are you looking at your screens to determine where that is going to come from each day or each week? What is the number you can make on a regular or consistent basis? You want to find what you can do. Once you can find that, you can increase the size of the positions. You need to have that kind of certainty about producing the result. Build a rhythm with one stock. Follow its fluctuations. Buy it low and sell it high. Once you have that, you can start doing that with two stocks. The best producers are confident about producing some number within a certain range.

**A:**     I was developing that kind of methodology and knew how I had to be positioned. The momentum of that was broken over the past three weeks. I have to find individual stocks where I can get an edge on fundamentals and can make an outsized percentage of returns in these stocks. I don't want to use the past three weeks as the reason to reject this formula. That can get you into trouble.

**K:**   Sounds like you have the right idea. I still hear you as trying to get a handle on a methodology.

**A:**   I think I am always trying to evolve. But I do think my methodology of getting the idea and making the P&L, I understand how I need to do that. I have good information. If U.S. Steel goes up four and goes down four in a three-week period without fundamentals changing, more of the names in my space are crowded and aren't trading. There aren't a lot of people making money in these larger names. You do need to focus on small-cap stocks, but that puts you at the whim of movements in the markets. That is where you are going to make the most money.

**K:**   Anything else that is not working? Anything more that you need to do? If it is working, what is the evidence that it is working?

**A:**   The P&L tells you it is not working.

**K:**   Do you have an explanation for it? Is it the price of oil coming down, the Federal Reserve adjusting interest rates, the economy stabilizing?

**A:**   It's the size and timing of the positions. I got too big too soon. I need to adjust it. I should get bigger at the right time. That is the thing I must work on.

**K:**   Could you have seen this? Could you have reduced the size of your positions in response to macro events? Could you have played a risk management game and waited until the catalyst? Can you extract that lesson from this experience?

**A:**   I took down the portfolio, but obviously not enough.

**K:**   You still believed in it?

**A:**   Some are positions that take time to build up. My stocks aren't trading like Microsoft. Having high conviction and not being there for the event cost me money in the past. So this time I wanted to be there in time for the event. I stayed in those. It's not easy to get in and out. I am probably losing 75 cents on either side of that trade, 5 to 6 percent to get in and out. I am confident that these positions will eventually work, so I didn't get out of them. I want to keep the same methodology: getting an edge on particular names, which will be profitable over the long term.

**K:**   You need to reduce the losses while you are waiting for the catalyst. You have to find what works for you—making a decision about cutting positions when they aren't working and getting back into them before they are about to start working or after the catalyst. You want to have the position, but at the same time you want to cut the losses. These are contradictory impulses and you need to learn to reconcile the two so that you can play for profitability at the same time as you are willing to reduce the size of positions that aren't working or even take them off your sheets. Controlling the loss of money is a critical component of managing your portfolio in order to produce profitability.

Risk management is critical for trading success, and this discussion is evidence of how fear can undermine a trader's plans for profits and for preservation of capital. Some traders need to be coached to take profits so they don't give back their gains.

Alan made some of his losses back, feeling good and confident and moving money around in positions depending on his level of conviction. He was still disinclined to take profits, but at least was willing to talk about it to some extent. Other traders find that they get stuck in positions and that the market moves against them very rapidly, taking profits with it. Still others must pay closer attention to the market action of their stocks and keep paring down losing positions.

A case in point occurred in September 2004. One trader was short steel, which was going up because of momentum buyers and not because fundamentals were good. Overall he was not making much money, but was rationalizing his losses.

## Case Study on Getting Out of Winners Too Fast

The following interview with Dennis shows a different response to stress. Dennis has demonstrated an inability to hold on to winners because of anxiety.

**Kiev:**     I think a lot of trading errors have to do with stress and maladaptive responses to it, which result in mistakes. The development of mastery relates to better managing the psychological component of trading. Why do you get out when your shorts are finally working? Is it because you are functioning the way Daniel Kahneman says people do, taking more risk when things are going against them and less risk when the odds are in their favor?

**Dennis:**  It is human nature. The reason why I get out is because I don't like the stress.

**K:**        That should be while the market is going up against you. Why do you get out when your strategy is finally working?

**D:**        Everyone extrapolates the last data point going forward. You know how painful it is. The moment it is working in your favor you want to get out, because that is a stress reliever. You have taken all that pain. The first chance you get to escape the dungeon, you go for it. You have held on in there, accepting the pain because you don't want to lose any money, but you are building up a lot of tension inside and waiting for the opportunity to escape from the situation, even if you don't have to run, because the liberators have come and you can walk out casually. Even when you realize you can get it back and then some, you don't. You are not trying to play it for its maximum value.

**K:** Is this when you have been intentionally shorting it and it has been going up against you, or when you didn't expect it would go up and you stay short so as not to face your loss?

**D:** Probably the latter. The best thing to do is to realize that under stress you are making an emotional rather than an intelligent decision. When you have the desire to cut your losses and you can book a profit, as when a short is finally turning downward, book it. That's when you should go back to your thesis to remind yourself what got you into the position so that you will have more staying power.

**K:** So review of your thesis will enable you to overcome the natural tendency to get out of the position.

**D:** You taught me that. You taught me to ask the question, "What do you have to do to have more conviction so that you can stay with a position?" At the most stressful times, especially in a market that is quite volatile, you have to constantly refresh, at a minimum on a weekly basis, why you are in the positions you are in. The moment the market reverses direction and gives you a chance to get out, you want to get yourself out.

**K:** Does that approach work for you on the long side as well?

**D:** On the long side I am more willing to cut out when things aren't working because it is indicative of the market we were in from 2000 to 2004, that the lows keep going lower and lower. The shorts wind up still working if you can stick with them longer. I use a longer leash on the short side than on the long side.

**K:** Do you experience stress in the market? How is that affecting your game? What mistakes are you making?

**D:** I am going into something else without doing the work, like looking for the next-best idea without recognizing that just because my current ideas aren't working doesn't mean I should play in a different sandbox. Under stress, you assume the grass is greener somewhere else.

**K:** The criteria are less relevant in these situations?

**D:** That's the problem. When you are not under stress and are in control, you take a look at new ideas in a more relaxed fashion. When you are stressed, you feel the pressure to find more shorts because the market is getting killed, and you jump into things before you do the work.

**K:**     Do you think you act irrationally when you are under stress?

**D:**     Absolutely. We actually don't need any more shorts than we needed yesterday just because the market is going against us today. It is very hard to do the risk management side of the book with the patience side of the book. Those two things are diametrically opposed. That is a constant battle. Let's assume you're wrong on your timing. How do you balance managing risk with having patience in the idea?

**K:**     Who is the risk manager?

**D:**     I am. The only reason you would need a risk manager is because someone else is trading your capital and you don't know what they're doing. I know I am losing money. I don't need a risk manager. I am managing the risk and I don't want to lose. Taking shots is what causes problems. A risk manager could work best when he doesn't know the stories. He knows the numbers. You get biased when you know the stories. The release valve of that pressure is to say, "We can always get back in." No one can disagree with that. No matter how much stress you are under, you can always sell it and rebuy it.

**K:**     Why don't people learn that? Is it that they don't like to admit they are wrong?

**D:**     The problem is you know you are screwed when the fear of missing it is greater than the fear of losing money. You set yourself up for a problem. I had one of those this month. I did a lot of work on this thing and couldn't get there. Fifteen minutes before a company reported, I had to be there and they totally missed. You feel like a dog in front of a T-bone steak. You are waiting. You go for it and get sick.

     What happens when you are missing stuff? That becomes stress. If this market goes up 10 percent and we are net flat, then we missed it. That is a stress that isn't factored into the portfolio, but factors into your mind game. It is very difficult to manage.

**K:**     The way you manage it is to have a target so that you don't look at what you are missing, but are you playing your game? You have to know how much you can produce and then accept that. As long as you are doing what you are capable of doing, you are happy with that and aren't looking elsewhere as to what else you could be doing.

**D:**     Then that is irrelevant.

**K:**     If you are not satisfied with what you are doing, perhaps you have to set bigger targets and figure out how much more work and what kind of detailed work you need to do.

**D:**     I want to manage it based on what I *am* doing, not on what I am *not* doing. I agree with that. I also think, when you are down, you have to keep playing as if you are up 5 percent for the month. Once you are playing defensively you will miss every opportunity because you are trying not to lose money. That is when you are selling something that is up 20 cents when you thought it would be up $3 to $4. That's when you stop playing your game.

If you can stop the bleeding and still be aggressive by slowing down how fast you pull the trigger, maybe you first have to dot your i's and cross your t's.

One of the big stress relievers is understanding that the numbers are what they are. You have to realize that the performance is what it is. It's not shoulda, woulda, coulda. Today I can make the same amount of money I lost yesterday. Just because you don't see that many opportunities in new ideas today doesn't mean you won't see those ideas in the days ahead. Knowing not to play is the best way to go.

Dennis was trying to find the right balance between risk management and sizing his high conviction ideas in terms of his stretch targets. I suggested he do this on a stock-by-stock basis within the framework of daily and weekly profit targets, and he reduced his losses for the month to $700,000.

To counteract the emotions of euphoria and fear, you have to learn how to let your winners run and how to get out of losers quickly. This is not natural. It is more natural to take a quick profit on winners and to hold on to losers, hoping they will turn around. The counterintuitive move is go against the emotional tide and to cut your losses and prepare for the time when they are going to start working. Desire to make more money is a motivating force but must be balanced by good risk management principles.

## GUILT

Sometimes traders are ashamed about their emotional reactions to stress. They feel they should be stronger and not react emotionally, or that they should be able to overcome their reactions much more rapidly. This is especially true of macho men who have been raised to believe "boys don't cry."

Guilt is also magnified by any tendency toward perfectionism, where people feel that there is a correct way to cope with stress and that they have failed to handle the event as some others might. The pattern of guilt varies. At one extreme are those who do not seem to feel guilty at all but exhibit self-destructive behavior that suggests that they are suffering from guilt. At the opposite extreme there are very depressed traders who are inclined to blame themselves for things irrespective of what has happened.

For example, Sanjay was expressing a sense of guilt related to the stress of working long hours and taking work home even though his wife was supportive and didn't seem to feel that there was a problem. Still, Sanjay continued to feel guilty about not spending enough time interacting with her. Actually, he was anxious because some of his health-care services ideas weren't working. Instead of finding ways to manage his tension and improve his concentration, he had allowed himself to transfer his anxiety to personal aspects of his life. We discussed ways of managing his tension, learning to separate the wheat from the chaff in terms of ideas and framing his work in terms of the actionability of ideas and data points.

Other traders feel guilty but cannot share their experiences because they fear the reactions of others. So they conceal their feelings and stew about them. When they do talk about their experiences, they tend to feel even guiltier. Expressions of guilt lead to more conviction that they have done wrong, and this leads to a circle of repetitive distress.

Perhaps the most fortunate of the guilt bearers are those who feel less disturbed by their reactions and are able to express their guilt about their past experiences. These people are able to seek help for their distress and can begin working toward the resolution of it. They recognize how the persisting guilty feelings contribute to their low self-esteem and sense of inadequacy.

Dave, for instance, continued to feel guilty about a reactive call he made in response to a recent news release. He felt totally responsible for responding without thinking through the correct answer. We talked about the necessity of reviewing the event in order to learn from it and the importance of doing the necessary work before making recommendations. He realized that he was better off keeping away from making market calls until he has done his homework. Having discussed all that, Dave now needed to let go of his guilt and move on.

Guilt keeps you mired in the past. It is socially conditioned and operates as an attempt to say or do the right thing by accepting blame for what has happened. In this sense, guilt serves to get approval and the favor of others. Once you see this, you can begin to release it. You must relinquish responsibility for what has happened, surrender to the forces of the universe or the market or some higher power, and accept relief. In doing this, you can step beyond the self-absorption of guilt and begin to redefine and re-create your trading career.

## WORRY

Most traders understand the inherent danger of the markets. After all, there is a lot of money at stake. Given the risks, it is imperative that traders trade wisely—gathering the appropriate amount of information, making informed decisions, getting in and out of trades on time.

Manolo, a typical worrier, was a student of how the Federal Reserve impacts the market. In September 2004, with the rising price of oil, the presidential election, and the soft economic numbers, Manolo believed the Fed was going to raise interest rates again, but he wasn't clear about the direction of the market. So he was playing it cautiously. He didn't want to put too much risk on when there was that much uncertainty. Given these conditions, worry can actually be productive in that it helps motivate traders to trade responsibly. However, worry—like most of the other emotions associated with stress—can become a serious disruption to your trading strategy.

Simon was trying to build up his confidence to recommend larger positions in his space, moving from less than $5 million up to $10 million. The problem was the anxiety he'd face if there were bigger losses in the larger positions when the stock is going against him. While he recognized that profitability might be even greater, he hadn't yet developed the stomach for increased losses while waiting for the profits to materialize. This shows up as an excessive reluctance to size positions.

When you begin worrying about things that are beyond your control or when you are spending excessive amounts of time and energy worrying instead of taking action, this emotion has become a distraction, leading to a myriad of trading errors. Some traders become so consumed with trying to master their reactions to the stress that they become trapped by their own thoughts. They find themselves unable to stop thinking about their problems. They constantly worry. They mull over events, anticipating the worst. Therefore, they magnify their problems just by thinking about them. The more you see events through the perspective of your fears, the more stuck you are in a vicious cycle—you are forever seeing your life through the template of the past.

Again, this tends to reinforce a sense of inadequacy and insufficiency and leads to more efforts to maintain an image of competency. The more you think, the more you worry. Ultimately, the tendency to worry is built on top of a fear of losing, of being rejected, and of being faced once again with even more stress. Sometimes this takes the form of denial, where a trader fails to examine his performance to correct it and grandiosely assumes that, given the ease with which it is possible to raise money, he will start a hedge fund of his own.

This was the case with Edgar, who was trying to find out as much as possible from old friends about running his own hedge fund. He was hoping to raise $50 million. He believed his track record from Goldman Sachs, where he made a return of about 15 percent for two years in a row, proved that he could make money and that his poor performance at his new company was an aberration because of his analysts. Nevertheless, he wouldn't have given up the opportunity since he learned so much there.

Internally, traders are operating on the assumption that if they worry about the issue long and hard enough, it will magically resolve or eliminate itself. In the face of this kind of circular thinking, they are actually more likely to exhaust themselves and keep feeling disempowered.

Here a trader should be alert to any inclination to drastically alter his strategy before correcting what is wrong in his trading. In such a situation, he must first review his statistics to see what must be modified.

Sometimes traders think teaming up with others will dramatically solve their problems. A case in point: Jack and Alan thought they could complement each other. I thought it was probably premature for them to team up. It made sense for them to sit next to each other and work together on ideas while building up some trading statistics to see whether they might have more winning days than losing days in their combined ideas and a better win/loss (W/L) ratio than each is producing at the present time alone.

Jack seems to have no problem getting ideas from the Street. I don't know whether what he gets from Alan will elevate his short-term game, and I don't know whether Alan will benefit by giving up his trading and relying on Jack for his income. It seems as if they are both coming from a sense of frustration and are grasping at straws to improve their performance without looking at the trading dynamics involved in a partnership, which rarely works even when good people team up.

## ANGER

It might be surprising to some, but anger is actually a normal response to stress. You may become angry about the event that triggered your stress as well as angry that you were chosen for the fate that befell you. Try as you may, you cannot get away from persistent nagging thoughts about the unfairness of the experience or particularly angry feelings toward those who have done you wrong. These feelings may lead to resentment and a lack of trust in the people around you. Your sense of stability may have been shattered. The world may no longer be predictable or stable for you. In addition to your anger for what happened, you are undoubtedly exasperated by the persistence of symptoms. You may also become irate at the individuals whom you believe to be contributing to your stress.

Here is an instance of anger causing additional stress. Shaun and Carlos were experiencing some communication issues. Carlos would get very anxious about wanting his best ideas to be well represented in the portfolio, even at times when there were no catalysts. Shaun, who was more risk-averse and price-sensitive, was reluctant to do this, but he didn't give Carlos strong opinions as to his reasons for not acting on Carlos's ideas. This further frustrated Carlos, who felt that Shaun wasn't taking a strong stand and being clear about his reasons. Basically, both traders acknowledged that while Carlos was the portfolio manager, Shaun wasn't listening to Carlos's requests, resulting in frustration and anger for the two of them.

Both traders were feeling the stress of the failing relationship and allowing their emotions to affect the outcomes of their trades. To curb the frustration and handle the stress, Carlos had to manage the process since Shaun kept wanting to hand over authority to him. He recognized that he had to teach Shaun how to communicate with him so that they could take their game to a new level. They needed to define a set of criteria about positioning and sizing that they were both comfortable with. They needed to create questions to routinely ask about their portfolio in a review of it several times a week, and they needed to develop an open discussion about their difficulties in communication.

Fortunately, Carlos and Shaun had already taken the first step—admitting their anger and that it needed to be resolved. For some traders, anger can become such a prominent symptom of stress that others find it hard to recognize the distress and vulnerability; all they see is the rage. It is the presence of anger that often initiates and perpetuates depression and anxiety.

Sometimes the anger is directed toward the risk manager. As we saw in Chapter 1, Stuart was disillusioned, angry, and low in morale because he believed that he couldn't recognize his portfolio now that he had to reduce the amount of capital he was putting at risk. He believed that he wasn't violating his contractual obligations by being down 5 percent and pointed out that his statistics had improved since his drawdown peak in May. I encouraged him to hang tough and try to build some P&L with the smaller portfolio. Then, when he started making money, he would likely get an increase of capital. The problem, of course, was that his stocks have not done well.

There is a continuum of behavioral patterns associated with anger. Some people are overcome and made powerless by anger. Others are comfortable with anger and are able to express it quite readily in a healthy way. At its most extreme, some traders are so incapacitated by anger and bitterness that they cannot let go of resentment toward certain people.

Spence was one such trader. Spence was a very conscientious guy with an inclination to become uptight and stressed out when things were getting difficult. He took his stress out on others by being very demanding and critical. It didn't really matter who experienced the brunt of his rage—other traders, limo drivers, travel agents. However, he saw that this was becoming a problem and admitted that he needed to get it under control. Spence was an excellent candidate for anger management therapy, and at least he was willing to admit his need for help.

Less troubling to others but still problematic to themselves are those whose lives are dominated by excessive efforts to control their angry feelings. If you identify with this description, on the surface you appear impervious to feelings and are highly controlled. You may have considerable difficulty in expressing your anger. You are gripped by a fear of losing control, and may tend to avoid others. While extremely sensitive to angry feelings, you find yourself trapped by your rage, which may be converted into depression, sulking, sarcasm, and cynicism.

Some people are more in touch with their anger. Try as they may they cannot banish the negative and vengeful feelings that obsess them. They cannot find a respite from negative thoughts that intrude into their consciousness during both waking and sleeping hours. Although they are consumed with bitterness, they are still able to function somewhat normally and are often motivated to learn how to deal with their angry feelings.

With practice it is possible to learn to express irritation, anger, and rage so you can become familiar with the behavioral and emotional responses of those emotions. (I'll discuss this in detail later on in this book.) This leads naturally to a greater ability to verbalize your feelings of anger without physical violence. You can then learn to share your feelings with others. Simply talking about your anger is often enough to dissipate it and expand an awareness of why a situation led to the automatic interpretation and reaction.

When you learn to express yourself without fear of retaliation or fear of injuring others, you can begin to see the value in allowing other emotions to surface and facing them. Moreover, you can see that you have the right to express yourself, to state what you are for and against, and to do so in an accurate and clear away without having to swallow your frustration. You don't need to build up tension and resentment. The more you can begin to express these feelings, the more you discover that you are capable of communicating other feelings.

Stress is inevitable—as are the emotions that go along with it. Given that trading is an extremely taxing and stressful career, no trader can continue to trade successfully under the influence of these emotions for any length of time. Stress will tax the body and mind and prove limiting to most traders. Sometimes stress is produced by multiple factors, and it is useful to explore them to see if you can get at a common denominator, which can then be modified.

I talked to one top analyst recently who was getting overwhelmed by various factors, even though he was pleased with his overall performance. He was upset because one analyst gave a single idea to five other analysts, creating a duplication of efforts. "Jeffrey doesn't seem to get it," he said. He was also annoyed at not being included in the loop regarding new ideas in venture capital, and by not having more than a very small percentage of commission dollars being allocated for the research process.

Making a conscious effort to stay focused, he went out fewer nights and took some time off to prepare for the end of the year.

## EUPHORIA

Not all the emotions associated with stress are bad, and there is stress associated even with good events in our lives. Weddings, promotions, and births are all very stressful events. In the same way, trading stress brings both bad and good emotions. Unfortunately, those good feelings can get in the way of your trading success just as much as the bad ones.

Often traders who are doing really well become overconfident, begin to take unnecessary risks, and fail to do the necessary work. In general, big wins lead some traders to abandon the discipline and trading strategy that helped them succeed in the first place.

In reviewing the work of Todd, the trader whose story began this chapter, it turned out that he had planned to get out of a long position when the market hit a certain high. Instead he got euphoric at that point and held on, only to see his profits disappear in the next turndown. He admitted to having some anxiety as he began to have some success. He generally tended to get "more stringent" and his portfolio got "very tight" when he was doing well. However, he might not take profits when he should (when stocks hit his profit target) and he got distracted by new ideas rather than concentrating on the ones that he had. He realized that he would have to stay on strategy the next time so this didn't happen again.

I suggested that he start keeping a diary of his trades, his subjective experiences to the markets, and the kinds of adjustments that he thought were most appropriate to build a track record and develop some "observing ego" about his trading that he could refer to in the future. This would give him some objectivity during his trades and help him control his trading.

In this way, he could review how his emotions were influencing his trading decisions. Todd and I also talked about ways of monitoring his anxiety so as not to be overwhelmed by his employer. He decided that he would try doing yoga six days a week to gain greater control over his anxiety. He also went on a raw produce diet for two weeks to help put him in right frame of mind.

Another example points to the same pattern. Bowen was upset about losing a good chunk of the money he had made recently. We talked about this to identify some of the reasons for his reversal. It seemed he was feeling fairly confident after the preceding month and didn't take some of his positions down. He started to lose, and then got into a defensive mode watching a variety of positions go down even while he was paring down his value at risk (VaR). He became so defensive and paralyzed that he missed a whole bunch of positive trades that he had identified. He just sat there and watched his P& L tumble 6 percent in one night. He missed the biggest up move. Now he lacked the confidence to get back in and was spending a lot of energy beating his chest, focusing on the past, and bemoaning how he had given up a good part of his year.

The pattern is always the same. If you don't stick to your strategy and you instead allow your emotions (either good or bad) to affect your trading decisions, you will fail to maximize your trading potential.

# CHAPTER 3

# The Dangers of Trading under Stress

### How Do Attempts to Handle Stress Create Problems for the Trader?

*A* *lexander was trying to learn how to manage a portfolio, to focus on high-conviction ideas, and to manage the risk in his positions better. He had trouble in the bear market of 2004, which was roiled by uncertainty about the Federal Reserve raising interest rates, rising oil prices, the continuing turmoil in Iraq, and doubt about whether the economy was improving. He was facing a dilemma between trading big-cap liquid stocks versus trading small-cap illiquid stocks that weren't being followed by very many people.*

*Under the mounting stress, Alexander realized that he was getting out of high-conviction ideas too early, but he then started overcompensating and getting too big too fast. Because he was thinking with his emotions instead of using a plan, he was not recognizing when his trades were losing money. He therefore kept rationalizing why he held on to losers. He was tense and anxious and reluctant to cut positions. The stress pushed him into a pattern of inflexibility that led to even more losses.*

Let's face it. Even at their best, the markets are stressful. Trading is a career that triggers anxiety, and unfortunately, anxiety often leads to maladaptive behaviors. This in turn influences the quality of trades and leads to problematic or defensive trading patterns. Most traders, under stress, are inclined to make mistakes. And given that traders are under almost constant stress . . . well, you can see the problem.

## TRADING DESPITE STRESS

The persistence of underlying feelings of self-doubt and insecurity leads to a constant need to keep down anxiety levels, and then this becomes the root of a variety of phobic and obsessive defensive patterns that are often intensified by subsequent stressful experiences. Many traders live in anticipation of further chaos and gain strength from a variety of rituals that work only temporarily. As a result, the trader learns to feel vulnerable and unprotected and may be less resilient in handling further stressful events.

Let's look at one trader's experiences by way of illustrating this concept.

### Case Study in Trading High-Conviction Ideas Despite Stress

**Kiev:**      As I understand your main issue, you want to size your high-conviction ideas before the events that you are waiting for, but you have to figure out how to manage the risk while you are doing it.

**Stanley:**   My first six months here, I overtraded a lot and we talked about not being in the catalyst positions when the catalyst came and then missing out on the opportunities. In the second time period, the past six months, especially the second portion of it, I wanted to be in my catalyst opportunities. If you have conviction in those ideas, you should be there for them. So I agree: It's an art of molding those two aspects; together they make up the methodology to be successful both in risk management trading and in maximizing profitability.

**K:**         How do you think you handled that critical time? Were you able to keep your losses down?

**S:**         As the whole market turned over, I went back and looked at what I did. At that point I pared back my portfolio, yet I also left very large positions and my high convictions on the sheets.

**K:**         Were things going against them at that time?

**S:**         No, at that time things were going with them. A good example of this is some Asian mining company I own. The financials were Friday and then yesterday there was a big catalyst. Since then, the stock has gone up 20+ percent. I did get bigger. I kept on buying after the catalyst, and then I kept on buying today.

**K:**         How many shares did you have?

**S:**         At the peak I had close to a million shares in the stock. It was about $5.

**K:** Did you get out on Friday or Thursday?

**S:** I got down to about 350,000 shares and then I built the position back up before the catalyst and now I am up to 725,000 shares.

**K:** Is it still working? Do you want to get bigger?

**S:** Yes. I did buy some more today.

**K:** Where is that now?

**S:** Almost at seven, and so I think there is going to be some overhang there. We are going to sell a little bit before we get to seven and then look to add on a pullback. Eventually I do think it's a $10 to $11 stock.

**K:** Where would you get out?

**S:** I would get out on the downside. I don't think this stock should go below $5.50 Canadian any more because a lot of the risks that people were nervous about have gotten better. The selling pressure is over and done with. I would have to question myself if the stock got back below about $5.50.

**K:** So if you got down, would you get out or cut your position down?

**S:** I would cut it down some more and then try to figure out why there was still selling left in the position. I have got to ask myself: "Am I right or am I wrong about this position?" I'd probably sell a quarter to half of what I bought. The next catalyst really isn't until the middle of September. I think this catalyst has brought enough momentum that it's going to continue to move back up.

**K:** It's almost like once you get a range you can write it up—kind of a profile.

**S:** The trading range of the stock in order to know when you should buy it lights up and adds back so that you build up the P&L within that position. Then you know if all of a sudden something else happens, and you get bigger because you have already built up that P&L, which is . . .

**K:** Each stock has its own footprint, and it just gets bigger and more information has more meaningful events. Your view is: "I don't care what anybody says. I am going to buy here, and it's good for three or four points and then we are going to start getting out." Maybe it's going to go up some more. But that's more fantasy thinking or hope than it is understanding the behavior of the stock. With that kind of information, you sort of know how each stock functions.

**S:** Right, and it's capitalizing on being able to trade that even though it's a big catalyst—a very high-conviction idea.

**K:**  To begin the value of the number or the target—that's really all you are concerned about, which means keeping the losses down and maximizing the wins. All that filters back into the pathway, which is how much money you can make on a given day. On some stocks you can make more; on others you have a risk. All these things help to make the number more precise. You know a particular stock never goes below $10 and it never goes above $20. Now it's at $10 and on its way to $20. It usually takes three months to get there. That means if I trade a million shares, I make 10 points, so that takes care of $10 million.

**S:**  Right. I have to ask, "Which stock am I going to be making my goal in today?"

**K:**  Not everybody approaches it that way. It is more like the mutual fund kind of mentality.

**S:**  This concept is a different way to think about it than most other hedge funds. Most funds are thinking more about putting good ideas on the sheets as opposed to reverse-engineering their P&L.

**K:**  They're not thinking about producing a result. The result is sort of the outcome.

**S:**  A more successful way is the reverse engineering of the result: What do you need to get there as opposed to will you get the result? That's what I think is unique about this approach.

**K:**  To have higher conviction means better ideas and to have better ideas you need more analysts and digging in deeper. So you start adding analysts to help get a little more confident about the ideas in order to make money. What are some other ideas to have? Your highest-conviction idea—what's that?

**S:**  My highest-conviction idea is in aluminum. In my book it's right now at $3.5 million.

**K:**  What's the price?

**S:**  It's about an $8 stock; it's going to be a $16 stock at the end of the fourth quarter. So it's a little way off, but I think there are multiple catalysts in between to get it there.

**K:**  Every time you get more conviction because another catalyst has happened, that proves you could raise your target to $6 million.

**S:**  Yes. The problem here is, it's not a very liquid stock. It's hard to buy even if there is a merger happening between two companies that I think is going to improve the liquidity. Once that liquidity has improved, I am going to buy more. You have two smaller-cap companies and they merge together; they become a mid-cap company and trade at a larger market cap. It gets into a lot of value; it gets on people's radar screens and all of a sudden it goes from trading 100,000 shares a day to trading 300,000 to 400,000 shares a day.

**K:** What's the risk/reward profile?

**S:** It could go down to six bucks. I want to increase the size, but I don't want to get too big too fast and have too many shares; and there is enough catalyst where I think I am going to be able to get involved on days when there is more liquidity.

**K:** Do you have any low-conviction ideas that are using up time and money?

**S:** Within my space, for better or worse you're at the whim of what the commodity is doing that day: what the dollar does, and why is this stock up 4 percent and why is this stock down 4 percent today? No real reason, my point being I do have some shorts in here that I don't think have much upside. I don't have any real reason to be shorting them other than to have some shorts against some of my high-conviction longs. They are just there as hedges. The volatility in a lot of these names has been really huge for no reason other than the dollar is up or the dollar is down. Just to have those in the portfolio helps on bad days.

**K:** Does it cost anything to be in a low-conviction idea? Does it cost you time or energy?

**S:** I think so.

**K:** What's the reason to stay in?

**S:** It's a short that I don't think is going higher. The question is, should you have any position in it and then look to just jump on it when it breaks at the right time?

**K:** If you hold on to some of these names with no reason, you weaken your discipline. It tends to foster a kind of casualness, a sloppiness. There may be some other reason. I am just thinking of it in terms of if you really start looking closely: "I am in this for this, and I am hoping to get this; to get this, I need to get twice as many shares. This one is going down. There are three catalysts; as the catalysts start working and it goes down, I am going to short more." So you build your lens for making decisions as to what you have: "When it again meets the criteria, we are going to get back in." This is just a way of strengthening your methodology. You know there is a high-conviction idea: Could you have a bigger position? "Well, no, I can't; there is no liquidity." How about this one? "In this one there is plenty of liquidity." Well, could you be twice as big, and are there good reasons to be? That's kind of what I am getting at. "This way I have got 20 positions, and 10 of them are strong enough. Seven are medium strong; well, the other three are just there because they are legacy positions." That is what I am looking at.

S:      I understand that.

K:      You want to become very focused in doing this. This is sharp-shooting. What I am getting at is: The more you do this, the more demanding and the more rigorous you get. The more rules you have as to what constitutes the justification of being in a position and what justifies getting bigger and at what point you're going to get out, the better you can do. You map it out and you have a game plan and you play that game plan out. Trading is stressful. It's going every which way, and the more you have a plan and follow the plan, the more you can ride through the stress. You are not affected by the market or affected by what everybody is doing. You know exactly where you are going. So it's a plan to deal with intrinsic uncertainty.

S:      It has to be stock-by-stock specific.

K:      You take that money and put it in one that you have high conviction in. Five hundred thousand dollars is a lot of money.

S:      I agree.

K:      You look at it and say, "Okay, there is no reason to be in this." You get out, and all of a sudden you become more active in managing. While it looks like nothing, it actually has given you more control over what you're doing. Now you are going to look at other things in the same kind of way—"Okay, this could be bigger"; "Okay, there is no reason to be in this." So you start moving for real reasons. You are watching each position. That becomes your task. You know more about these stocks than anybody else.

As Stanley illustrates, the various dilemmas facing the trader in balancing his risk management principles with his trading thesis along with his notions about sizing high-conviction ideas can create a significant amount of stress—all of which may only serve to magnify the dilemma.

Stress becomes dangerous when traders turn it, and the emotions associated with it, into negative trading patterns. By learning how your interpretations of and reactions to stress are creating these obstacles, you can then begin to reframe your attitude toward stress and trade in a more effective way.

## AVOIDING THE STRESS

Sometimes the initial symptoms of stress appear to be reasonable responses to the event—confusion, bewilderment, psychic numbing. Because many traders do not recognize that what they are experiencing is a natural response to stress, they are often embarrassed or humiliated when their symptoms first begin to occur. Even though they may be mature adults, too many of them believe they will be perceived as weak or childish if they reveal their feelings. They may even try to hide their symptoms. Sometimes they think there is "something terribly wrong" with them and that they are "losing their mind" or "going crazy."

The ever-present distress of disturbing thoughts and the possibility that they may recur in relation to certain events leads traders to further curb their behavior and to avoid those events. This is known as persistent avoidance or numbing of responsiveness.

At its most extreme, some traders get out of trading altogether. Commenting on this trend in the world of macroeconomic traders, one experienced trader, David, was quite explicit about how difficult it was, how badly people were doing in the year 2004, and how so many were thinking of leaving the profession altogether.

## Case Study: Difficulty in Avoiding Stress

**Kiev:** You have told me that 3 percent of the time you're making money. What do you mean by that?

**David:** You've got to be in there, but you can't be in there losing. One major firm was down on their $4 billion fund. Their $2 billion fund was up 9 percent and then they gave back five last month. Do you know how much that is? That's like $400 million or $500 million they lost last month. So the key is to hang in there and don't be too stupid. I saw one guy who had been away for a while and came back for a few days and was like "I'm done with this. There is nothing to do." I could tell by hearing it in his voice. In a year like this you have to have some perspective. It's been like drawing blood from a stone.

**K:** Most guys are talking about how they wish the year was over. I don't know whether starting a new year makes any difference.

**D:** Historically, for me, if I can weather these periods plus or minus 2 or 3 percent, it's been fine. That's what we have been doing.

**K:** Guys who aren't experienced kind of think they are in the wrong game or they're getting out. Guys who have been here before say you've got to ride it out until you get better.

**D:** If it lasts another six months, guys are going to kill themselves; people will leave. I have seen it before.

**K:** How long does it take for those guys to come back, or do they never come back?

**D:** A year or two after the next period when things are better.

**K:** People stay with those memories.

D:    They sell the low and buy the high. I don't mean to be glum about this, because I don't know that this is going to play out the way I think it is. Today I am just doing little trades—five lots, ten lots—tiny little nothings. I have lost money on most of them. It doesn't add up to any substantial money, though.

K:    Just to stay in the game, just to keep that feeling.

D:    It's hard to know what to say—I suppose just stay in there mentally, do little things right, and hopefully you see a surprise stock move up. It really is important to focus in on two or three things that we think are right and not get distracted also by all the other things.

K:    How about a guy who trades 30 different ones?

D:    I don't know. He is probably doing badly this year. There is too much stuff going on.

K:    Does that strategy ever work?

D:    It could work when everything is working, but when nothing is working it doesn't work. Like last year everything worked—every single thing that he did.

K:    So you stay concentrated on a few things?

D:    It's the *not* doing that saves you. The key is to hang in there when it's not clear. When it gets clear it's a lot easier. So when it's not clear, the goal is to try not to lose too much money.

K:    Are people more likely to fail because they hold on to their losers?

D:    It's also holding on to a belief system that may have expired.

K:    Are you saying guys are too attached to it?

D:    To the methodology, not necessarily to the idea. They understand this better now and are trying to get more control. Of course, what has that led to? It's led to a lot less trading, of course. If you are not sure about how your methodology applies to something, you trade less. So that's the key thing to realize: Basically, what you're doing isn't necessarily what you've always done. It isn't necessarily working; it's not necessarily right. You know what? This can change on a dime. You also have to be sensitive to it all of a sudden working again.

K:    Do you have to keep looking for what's new, or do you just have to keep waiting for the opportunity to do it?

D:    Both. The game changes, but all of a sudden it can go back to the way it was, once everyone has stopped believing in it. People will get burned out, especially people who have already made $50 million. Why would you bother with it?

K:    By burned out, do you mean it doesn't work, and then they don't want to reinvent themselves because it's too much struggle?

| **D:** | Too much struggle; it's hard. |
|---|---|
| **K:** | There is no satisfaction in reinventing yourself? |
| **D:** | It could take years or months of work. |
| **K:** | How about some of these guys who are doing it until they are 90? |
| **D:** | It's the same thing. But that's Warren Buffett, who is worth $30 billion. I mean the number of guys like Warren Buffett, Steve Cohen, and Julian Robertson is small. |
| **K:** | There are not too many. |
| **D:** | That's the whole point. You only get to be an old guy in the business if you're a guy— |
| **K:** | —who is willing to keep transforming. |
| **D:** | Right! Take a look at some of the guys who never really were thought to be that bright, but all of a sudden had made $20 million for themselves. So they probably say, "I have made this $20 or $30 million or it's in the fund, and this is 10 times more than I thought I would make in my whole life. It's too hard; I will go home." A lot of guys who rolled during the boom feel it's way too stressful. |
| **K:** | It's a stressful job. |
| **D:** | And there are long periods of potentially no return. I am flat this year, and I've made no money so far. So I have gone nine months and made no money. I have my investors telling me they want to keep putting money in. They think I am doing a great job given the environment. I don't see I am going to do anything with it. Do they just want to give me the fees off of the money? What's the point of that? And then all of this is made more difficult by the fact that there is just too much money in the game now. |
| **K:** | Too many hedge funds? |
| **D:** | Yeah. |

What David was saying was that only the strong, focused, and committed survive when the markets go through a tough period. There are not many traders who can hold on for a long stretch and remain mentally alert for the next upward swing.

In such times, the trader is besieged by an onslaught of symptoms and soon learns to avoid what he deems the anxiety-producing situations or even his own thoughts about the situation.

Most traders, however, are unaware of their avoidance or how problematic it is going to be. This pattern often generalizes to an even broader range of stimuli until some people find themselves totally immobilized by constant fear.

As a result of the stress, some traders avoid getting involved in almost everything for fear they will experience a repeat of the original symptoms. This is especially true regarding situations that are similar to the original ordeal. The more they avoid, the more anxiety and tension build. Instead of lessening the symptoms, avoidance actually leads to mounting tension and magnified fear.

Underneath the avoidance behavior is generally a fear of failure, an uneasiness about rejection, and a concern about inducing the original anxiety. As a result of the reactivation of anxiety under a variety of circumstances, you tend to continuously restrict your behavior until you are finally locked into a prison of your own making. Then, you are effectively living in the past rather than in the present moment.

The problem is that you are neither comfortable letting go of the self-protective routines of the past nor comfortable in dealing with the uncharted future. Your characteristic ways of trading keep alive the same anxiety-ridden perspective that was imprinted at the time of the loss.

You may shut yourself off from others and may be overly sensitive to the remarks of others. This further accentuates your desire to avoid involvement and leads to enhanced feelings of loneliness and abandonment. So, avoidance itself creates its own stress.

Of course, the ultimate avoidance is one of noncommitment to yourself and your trading vision. This demonstrates itself as a refusal to pledge yourself to an outcome. You won't take on anything without certainty or guarantee, preferring to maintain stability and a sense of security by following repetitive routines or sidestepping situations that may trigger anxiety. Your whole life reflects your imprisonment to your own thoughts.

You may believe you are unable to do certain things because you have lost your nerve and are afraid you will fail. You anticipate anxiety everywhere and are good at finding excuses to shun situations and activities. This may even take on phobic proportions to the extent that you avoid all social contact and relationships with others.

Another pattern of avoidance arises when you try to cover up or mask something about yourself that you don't want others to know. It doesn't really matter what it is. If you are trying to create a false impression of yourself, if you are hiding something about yourself, you are being inauthentic, less powerful, less real, and less alive than you are able to be. As you free yourself of your need to appear other than who you are, you will become more powerful, effective, and engaged in the processes of your life. The more you can face the conflicts and challenges before you, the less need you will have to appear to have it all under control.

Much avoidance consists of the denial of reality. You may be refusing to admit to the challenges, failures, insufficiencies, and distances between where you are and to what you have committed. Once you begin to face the problems that are present and view them as opportunities to create your life, you will find more ways to master those challenges. To do this, you must face the truth about the circumstances rather than denying them. You must first acknowledge your vulnerability. Tiptoeing up to the brink, you must peer over the edge of the abyss and live in a world that, by definition, is uncertain. You have to allow your objective to define the actions you will take rather than being governed by your automatic defensive patterns from the past.

---

**Avoidance Behavior: Quiz and Exercise**

- Have you experienced a trade that induced such negative symptoms that you now characteristically avoid even thinking about it?
- What are the repetitive thoughts that you keep replaying in your mind in relation to this experience?
- What repetitive or ritualistic patterns of behavior do you engage in?
- Consider what symptoms of anxiety you regularly experience when you approach the avoidance situation.
- How can you let go of the obsessive, repetitive, or negative thoughts? Let them all drift into your mind; then make a list of them, and finally visualize yourself putting them all in a jar. Now, imagine emptying the jar into the trash.

---

## CREATING A SOCIAL PERSONA

Stress and its related symptoms can also lead to defensive patterns of behavior or social personae that are like acts or routines that become characteristic ways of functioning. These defensive acts are subtle ways that people use to try to cover up feelings of incompleteness or inadequacy in an effort to look good and minimize stress. Let's examine a few of the more common defensive postures induced by stress.

### Helplessness

Stressful events may undermine your confidence in yourself and lead you to rely more on the opinions of others. They may intensify your sense of dependency and need for approval. And then all of these factors may operate to hinder you from pursuing your own objectives.

Needing to minimize your difficulties and deny the pain of an experience, you may compromise the truth rather than face facts as they are. To the extent that you perceive everything as a potential source of anxiety, you are inclined to interpret everything in terms of possible problems. People and events are not seen for what they are. You perceive a hidden meaning in everything and therefore mask everything, and the simplest event may be embellished and distorted. You function as if there is something of which you are ashamed. You are reluctant to admit to things for fear of embarrassing yourself.

You may sugarcoat much of what you want to say, anticipating the worst from others. You edit your conversations in terms of what you think will sound right or correct and thus end up feeling somewhat compromised in your relationships and vulnerable to the opinions and reactions of others.

Frank is a trader who exemplifies many of the problems associated with helplessness. He wants to create his own fund but constantly tries to put the responsibility for doing this on someone else. He says he is looking for support, but he actually wants someone else to do it for him. He doesn't seem to have the same degree of conviction and confidence about doing the mundane, everyday things as he seems to have when it comes to trading. Frank exudes a nice-guy image but deep down lacks the kind of confidence needed to create something bigger. In fact, confidence has been a lifelong issue. As such, he needs some heavy-duty coaching to take psychological ownership of the process. He needs to focus on digging in deep and coming up with a real plan of his own rather than expecting someone else to come up with the plan. After more discussion, he finally understands that he needs to design and take ownership of his future goals.

When you become stuck on negative experiences and thoughts of a loss, you disempower yourself. Pay attention to thoughts, because what usually comes next is a belief that other people know best what you should do. This goes right along with the inclination to minimize the value of your own thoughts. Consider:

- To what extent are you reluctant to trust your own instincts and to make decisions based on your own desires?
- How much do you take responsibility for your own needs?
- Do you think that others should take care of you because you can't take care of yourself?

I can't tell you how frequently I encounter this problem in my work with hedge fund managers. Analysts who report to portfolio managers run into this issue more often than most other people, and it usually provides an opportunity to challenge people about taking more responsibility for their own behavior, their own expectations, and how things work out for them.

Do you have any thoughts related to the belief that you are helpless? This is especially common in the earliest stages of stress when you are most anxious and focused on the past. Take a close look at yourself. Go to the "Helplessness" questions that follow and answer each in a short paragraph. Don't worry if your answers suggest you are needy. You are just beginning to take control of your actions again, so it's important not to be too hard on yourself.

## Helplessness: Quiz and Exercise

- How much are you governed by a need for approval such that you are reluctant to pursue your own objectives?

- Do you feel trapped by the expectations of others? Are you too frightened to pursue your own objectives?

- How much do you feel overwhelmed by the stressful nature of your trading career and by any one particularly stressful event?

- Did you decide after a certain loss that your career was over or that there was nothing you could do to empower yourself?

- Do you blame circumstances and others for your continuing difficulties?

## Helpfulness

Another one of the most commonly occurring defensive stances takes the form of helpfulness. You may take the lead in trying to control situations. You may be quick to teach others what is the best way to do things. You may find fault with their ideas and correct them for "their own benefit." You may cite your own experiences to prove a point without realizing how patronizing this is and how much resentment you are creating. You may not be as helpful as you think you are.

Consider Madeline, a bright woman interested in improving her performance. Her greatest strength is her ability to work alone and her high energy level, but she is a bit weaker in her capacity to read interpersonal signals. She has become increasingly self-conscious and apologetic in her efforts to adapt and to anticipate what others want rather than concentrating on her work and waiting for specific instructions. She has potential—if only she would slow down, take a deep breath, and wait for requests. She needs to focus more attention on preparation instead of giving in to her anxiety to please and trying to be helpful.

Another example of a trader who is struggling with helpfulness is Mitchell. I have been talking to him about time management, prioritizing tasks, and not getting too caught up in the demands and issues that others are making on his time. Since this is eating away at valuable time that needs to be spent elsewhere, we discussed some practical ways in which Mitchell could get past his inclination to always say yes.

I suggested that he allocate all of his tasks to a place on his calendar and then manage his time around this schedule. In particular, he would then have to schedule all impromptu conferences and meetings to a free time slot. This would help him to politely decline invitations that infringe upon his schedule.

Of course, there are also traders who battle this persona in a different light. They tend to have an overly exaggerated view of themselves and constantly try to help in areas where their advice or assistance is either unwanted or not needed. For example, Kai has been managing a large portfolio and now believes that he can take on a significant role in management. He has an exaggerated view of his own ability to understand the psychology of situations. In fact, he tends to believe that other traders come to him to resolve business issues or solve problems—a self-evaluation that is inaccurate in that other traders rarely ask him for this kind of help. This becomes a problem given that he is requesting new career opportunities. He thinks he would be good at managing relationships with Wall Street and acting as a representative to the company of the interests of certain portfolio managers. In this regard, the other traders may not actually give him the respect that someone in this position needs, and at the end of the day they may bypass him as a so-called weak suit. Again, his arrogance is evident when upon further discussion he begins to wonder whether he might be overqualified for the new position and whether the required travel would be worth his while. Indeed, Kai seems to have a strong desire to "be the man" and to have decision-making power rather than just reporting responsibilities.

Traders who battle with a helpfulness persona may in fact be controlling and manipulative. They may be unaware that they are not interacting with others in a mutually supportive way. And helpfulness can actually be a mask for aggressive feelings generated by the stress associated with wanting more success.

## Self-Pity

Self-pity is also a common defensive behavior in which you focus on the wrongs you incurred and anticipate that you will be victimized again. You are supersensitive to mere slights, and people are frequently put on guard by your sensitivity. You may even convince people that they are rejecting you when they are not. Unwittingly, you may manipulate other people into feeling guilty about *your* feelings.

Floyd has a problem with this kind of "chest beating." He has recently been too inclined to sell his stocks to take his profits and has suffered for it. He needs to get back to his original game by taking larger positions when he has high conviction and then trading around the position. He has to learn to stop bemoaning his fate after he sells a stock that proceeds to move up some more. This obviously only serves to distract him from his trading vision, because in fact, if he still likes the stock, he can always buy it back.

Of course, some traders take on this role because of the secondary gain associated with it. As victims, they benefit by being thought well of and feeling superior to others because of their capacity to suffer. While martyrdom appears to be problematic, they thrive on it.

Juan is suffering from a lot of negative thought processes about himself and his sector. He believes that he has no edge, that his stocks are illiquid, and that he does not have nor ever will have discipline. As a result, he holds things too long, especially when they are going against him, believing that they are likely to turn the moment he gets out of the positions.

He thinks if he holds things long enough they will eventually turn in his favor. Since he has no edge, he feels justified in trading stocks in many, many sectors. We counted trades in over 40 sectors, although he defended this by saying many of them were related. I had five recommendations for him:

1. Do not oversize too early. Build positions incrementally, and don't put on a full size at the start. Be careful about entry points, and have some thoughts about price targets and level of conviction.

2. Decide how much you are willing to lose in a trade. Plan stop-out points, put them on a spreadsheet, and have someone else monitor this to create a forced discipline.

3. Research algorithmic trading programs, which may enable you to get into small illiquid positions without stirring up the prices too much.

4. Reduce the number of sectors that you trade, especially groups where you lost significant amounts of money last year.

5. Try to size your high-conviction ideas in sectors and stocks where you have an edge.

Fortunately, Juan was willing to try some of these suggestions. After much discussion he agreed to put on stops in several positions. He also agreed to use $300,000 in losses as a reason to reduce his position size by half, and a partner was going to develop a mechanical system for identifying these trades so that he could monitor Juan's trading and remind him of what he had promised to do by way of risk management. By taking these steps, Juan was trying to take back responsibility for his trading and remove the mental baggage he had acquired with his "poor me" view of the world.

## Procrastination

Procrastination sometimes blends into passive-aggressive behavior where there is an unconscious intention to disappoint others or not comply with their wishes. You may be so fearful of making a mistake or of reactivating anxiety that you have learned to postpone action. The result is that you are never on time, don't finish things when you are supposed to, and are always putting things off. You are just a little too late getting in or out of a trade. The more you postpone action, the more tasks build up and seem insurmountable. The small task begins to weigh on you, and you are burdened by expectations. Soon others stop relying on you, and you are again back in your victim's stance, blaming others for not cooperating and the fact that things aren't going the way you think they should.

Other such passive-aggressive behaviors include misinterpreting communications so that you appear to be interested when you aren't and rejecting the help you invite by complaining. You ask others to give you advice—and then reject the advice. You look for opportunities to be cynical. These patterns may reflect the fact that you are looking for the right thing to do but are averse to committing yourself because of the stress associated with the solutions. You are both helpless and controlled, anxious to be assisted but hesitant to let go of the way in which you are already doing things. You cannot tolerate the stress of change.

Having been clobbered by stress, you are now trying to express various negative emotions in socially acceptable ways so that others won't know what you are feeling. Defensive behavior patterns like those mentioned earlier may enable you to cope indirectly with the stress of your trading career, but they also limit your creativity and self-expression. They box you into a fixed way of responding to events and reduce the amount of support and nurture you receive from others.

## COMPETING TO WIN

Another emotion that occurs as a result of the stressful trading environment is envy, and envy ultimately leads to competition. While competition can be beneficial in some arenas, it places attention on winning, not on action, and only reinforces a sense that you are not okay the way you are. When you can renounce competition, you let go of self-deception and self-doubt.

If you can give up your inadequacy, you will learn that whether you succeed or fail is not the point. It is the action that you have taken that matters. Your success or failure is only the start of the next step. In essence, your task is to keep moving forward.

When you find yourself envious of someone else or frustrated by another person's success, don't deny your feelings, but step back a bit and look at them from a different angle. Consider the following questions, and record your answers in a journal.

- What is this person doing that makes you envious? How is he doing it?
- How is he setting the pace for you?
- How is he demonstrating steps that can be learned?
- What lessons can be gleaned from his success?

There is value in periodically reviewing these journal notes to see what you can learn about yourself and how you can apply yourself to your objectives in a more focused way. Additionally, over time you will begin to see that the negative feelings of envy are transient and that gradually they pass. Learning this, you will know the next time you experience them that they are not permanent but will also fade over time and that perhaps you can gain greater personal insight into yourself and what you must do from examining your experiences.

The success of others paves the way for you. It provides opportunities. Envy and jealously are triggered when you are off-center. As such, they can be used as cues that you need to reformulate and recommit to your objective.

The key to handling envy, jealousy, and feelings of competition is to be who you are. Find your own tracks. Keep focusing on what you can do without being distracted. Accept the situation as a learning tool.

## Case Study in Handling Competition

In this dialogue, Darryl talks about the stress of macroeconomic trades, the characteristics of the successful trader, and what personality traits are needed for successful trading. He also discusses the need to tolerate uncertainty to be able to develop the variant perception and to think outside the consensus in the outlying trades and events. Darryl illustrates how a successful trader uses constructive steps to manage daily stress so he can continue moving forward whatever the market environment is.

**Kiev:** Many things going on in the world have made the markets a very uncertain place. I am looking at the situation in terms of how people adapt. How do they deal with it from a trading point of view? How do they deal with it from a structural point of view? How do they deal with it from a leadership point of view? Are there any people who have failed and then, based on what they have learned in their failure, are able to turn it around and produce a breakthrough? I have heard about one hedge fund manager who started with $100 million and went up to $500 million. He then lost everything, and now he is running $2 billion. People say he didn't ever change his strategy but he turned it around. There aren't too many stories of people who turned it around.

**Darryl:** I did that three or four years ago. The one thing that is always key is to reduce your expectations and don't get out of the markets. Don't take a break. Don't give up. Just trade smaller, a lot smaller. You know, the worst thing you can do is give up, because then you lose your feel; intellectually it kills you.

**K:** It's very hard to come back.

**D:** I have one position on, just a currency a quarter of the size than I normally would, because I think it's the right bet. There are so many different variables right now. I try not to stay out of the market but rather trade smaller, do a lot of research, and reduce expectations. Then just wait. The problem is that you have to be able to afford to wait. A lot of people can't afford to wait, especially guys who are day trading. I am trying to capture moves that are three to five months, and two months sometimes. For me, what happens in this environment is that the market doesn't want to pay me for those ideas over that period of time. So I try to shorten up my swing. I will book profits on something after a three-day move, when ordinarily that would just be a time I would be getting longer.

**K:** What are you waiting for?

**D:** Waiting for the big move, but now that I know this is happening, last month I was down half a percent. For me that is nothing. Last year in March I was up 6 percent; I was up 8 percent in September. I was basically flattish the rest of the year up or down half a percent, whatever it was. The point is I am not going to make 8 percent a month now. It's not there, so I basically am very comfortable floating around the zero line until the opportunity comes. I have been plus or minus 2 percent all year. I am very comfortable in that mode of plus or minus a few percent. I mean I would like to be plus, but as I said to you a few weeks ago, this is a time like five years ago when I would have been down a huge amount last month and I wasn't. I took precautions; I was defensive. I did all the things that you would normally need or want to do. I think that's very poor. You can't play your old game being in an environment where that game doesn't exist. So the key thing is to acknowledge that. My trading volume is down probably 60 to 70 percent from last year. It's down that much because how can I take risks in this environment?

**K:** If you don't have a cushion, is there pressure to perform?

**D:** You have to let that go. In one of my accounts I am up $700,000 on the year. That is terrible, but deep down I am flat. That is better than being down $5 million or $10 million, pressing it on something that isn't there. So that is the key. The key is to realize that it is more difficult than how you ordinarily used to make money. The structure of your thought process is not the same. So, for instance, I had an edge on some data. I knew the Japanese gross domestic product (GDP) was going to come out softer. It blew everyone away in terms of how soft it was. It was beyond even what I expected. I had a big position beforehand. At the end of the weekend I was thinking this was it. The next day it reversed itself and now the end is even higher than where it was after that number. The market is bigger than me, but also I play to make money.

**K:** So your usual strategy isn't working?

**D:** Sometimes it is and sometimes it isn't. So there is no consistency in it. So if there is no consistency, if that method that I use is applied randomly, you have got to be very careful and trade very small. What also happens is I tend to start putting on a slightly different hat. I start putting on more of a contrarian trading hat, where I will say okay, everyone is massively long Canadian dollars because they think the bank in Canada is going to raise interest rates next week. I think the data here is softening. Well, that would force someone to be long Canadian.

**K:** What is the next step?

**D:** After the rate hike maybe I will consider shorting Canadian dollars because everyone will have bought on that idea. So I have to take more potshots. Maybe I can pull a half a percent or a percent out of that. I will do that kind of thing until that game becomes clearer. This happened in the middle of 2000. I was down a chunky amount of money. I took a few weeks off to clear the mind. I came back and started trading a lot more and being involved very short-term in things to not lose my feel. I would see something and then it would go up, and I would take it off so I got into the habit of booking profits. I made $40 million in three months. You trade much smaller; you try to keep your powder dry so that you don't ever get in a position that you are down so much. If you are down 10 percent, you are dead. What are you going to do?

**K:**　　　You mean that psychologically it is impossible to recover when or if you are down 10 percent?

**D:**　　　It's hard to come back unless you're someone really special. Also look at the bottom line to see if you have enough in your own bank account to deal with this. You can't be relying on this to live. So my life didn't change at all in 1999 and 2000. I made enough money in my career that I can weather that storm, fortunately. So now to be flat on the year, although it's disappointing, it's not affecting my lifestyle.

**K:**　　　When you have enough experience, you know it's eventually going to start crystallizing?

**D:**　　　At some point, and it may take longer than I want.

**K:**　　　Is this tough for people to get into the macro game?

**D:**　　　I think the master traders can make money doing this. I think for lesser guys it's more difficult. You know because the macro community is full of a lot of these guys who are bigger thinker trend players. These markets are big, so anybody could be involved. They just stick to their view; they don't get out, and then they get too big. Macro is very seductive. You can have an idea. You think you really understand something, and you think you know, and you think you're right, and you just stick, and you get killed.

**K:**　　　This game is why people are great to play it.

**D:**　　　They're too intellectual.

**K:**　　　Do you think their intellectual ability allows them to get into it?

**D:**　　　Correct! I think that's part of the reason you don't have more traders. I probably made all the money in my career, starting in 1992 until now, in probably around five bets.

**K:**　　　How many bets have you made?

**D:**　　　Hundreds.

**K:**　　　You made hundreds of bets and you made most of your money in five?

**D:**　　　Correct! Meaning that if you weren't involved in the other bets you would never have seen the five.

**K:**　　　So did those five come out of being in the game?

**D:**　　　Yes, but being in the game is small, so that's why I said to my investors, "I will be plus or minus one or two or three, whatever. I will be near the zero forever until there is something real."

**K:**　　　You can't extract from that "I am going to be looking for those five bets"?

**D:**　　　That's over the years since 1992.

**K:**　　　Are you saying that other activity gets you into the big bets? You just want to keep busy?

**D:**     It gets you into the big bets—that's the whole point. I don't need to be busy looking for them. So now I have a quarter position on this thing. If this were a big bet I would have on eight times the size. All the money has come from these five or six bets. I know when they're real, and I was there in October of 2000. All of a sudden I was making $5 million a day after being down. No one understands how this game works. Every single guy made his money that way. I bet I could sit down and account for George Soros's wealth over the past 10 years just on his bets. There are things that become clear every once in a while, alternating with vast periods of confusion and pain-in-the-butt just trading bull. Then there are periods where there is clarity. It's hard, because then you are not sure whether it's real now or not. Is it part of the mass of nonsense?

**K:**     I am looking at this from a psychological angle, and if you kind of look at yourself as much as you could, what would you say were the psychological characteristics that accounted for the successes? Persistence, caution, thoughtfulness, or willingness to be in the water but then wait for the opportunity . . .

**D:**     That's it—you've got it. You have to have a backer that has the patience. What messed me up here my first few years was that there was no acknowledgment of the structure of macro. So I was never going to make 2 percent a month. I never said I could. I was going to be zero, and then I was going to have a 10 percent month. There was never any comfort with that.

**K:**     Did other macro traders experience the same thing even though the trades may have been different trades?

**D:**     No, they would have been pretty much similar. There were trades up there that I missed.

**K:**     Is there the ability to get bigger when you see the opportunities?

**D:**     You really have to know something.

**K:**     Can you expand on that?

**D:**     It's not like an equity trader who hears a tip from something or hears this and hears that and then passes it on; they can make $2 on the stock. That's not what this is. It never was that. I mean this is more about seeing things before other people, and then that is why the big macro guys have so much respect in general even if they lose money.

**K:**     What are the other keys to successful macro traders?

**D:**     The ability to really be able to scan markets and being able to change. Also being able to change your focus. If I said, "What did I do wrong this year?" the one thing that I did wrong was I did think months ago that crude oil could have a big run for technical reasons and for other reasons that I was reading. I never got involved. I never took the time to do all the work to have the comfort to have the position. That was a mistake. I really should have done that. Every time I have made chunky money it's been because I have done something that I had previously felt uncomfortable doing. So when I get over this discomfort, I am able to do well on it. It's a very weird thing.

**K:**   It's kind of like doing something new and really doing the work.

**D:**   That's exactly it.

**K:**   Have you got another example?

**D:**   This year was a chance for me to really dive into the oil. I knew it and I didn't do it. So I got penalized.

**K:**   Did it look like that going forward?

**D:**   That's when I know I am going to make money, and I am not there yet. I remember I get 300 e-mails a day. I read all of this. I have my notebook. That's all they do all day—sending ideas, looking at correlations. Some of it is technically based and some of it is fundamentally based. We are looking for outlying things that surprise you.

**K:**   In looking for the outlying idea—that puts you into the realm of cognitive dissonance.

**D:**   When I have a problem, it comes when I am living in a gigantic minority. Sometimes it's tiring and sometimes you just want to give up. You can live months and months in a minority. For instance, this year in June or July I went up to the trading floor my one time a year and I told the boss, "Everything is slowing down. Every piece of leading information, everything that I look at tells me the cycle is slowing down." Almost no other person in the world felt that. I was so in the minority—it was just me and three other people—that I couldn't even put the trade on, which was to go long at the bottom. It was too uncomfortable. I had been sitting there for months, and you know the cycle was at a very high level still and we were just turning down a little. We are not turning down the speed. That was the problem: It was still activity at a very high level. So basically the discomfort comes and a master trader will talk to you. You are basically always fighting the herd. Normally you can go against the herd. To go against 99 percent of them, maybe that's perfect because there is no one left to do it. The point is it wears on you and it can break you down and it forces you to miss it.

The point here is that Darryl consciously goes against the grain, looks for the variant perception, and feels very uncomfortable being the only trader who sees it. Nevertheless, he is secure enough to stick to his guns, and he tolerates the stress that accompanies being in the minority in order to come out ahead in the end.

## BEING INDECISIVE

A prominent emotion felt with stress is confusion. Traders can easily become overwhelmed with the decisions they face. This confusion can lead to indecisiveness (as well as extreme caution, perfectionism, and other problems that will be discussed later in the book). Indecisive traders wait too long before acting, or they can act too impulsively without enough information. They waffle on their decisions and second-guess themselves almost constantly.

Woody was one trader who came to me because he was concerned that he was becoming indecisive and uncertain. He had been doing well, trading in a fluid fashion and making money. He had a bigger net worth and was looking at things more objectively and taking profits in a few of his longs. He had been watching a few of his stocks go down in the past few days and decided that he would buy more when they came in. He tried to buy some stocks but couldn't, and the prices moved up, and he decided to back off. Basically, he stopped playing his own game, which was driven by fundamentals. Instead, he overreacted to the market and tried to make some short-term trades. He admitted that he was aiming to correct what he had failed to do the previous year, which was to ride out the full momentum of his trades.

I suggested that perhaps this was not the best time to try to learn how to correct for last year's failings but that he would be better served if he relaxed, went back to his original game, and got back in at whatever price whenever he decided the stocks were really starting to move. He might give up a point or two in the process by not being there beforehand, but at least he would be acting more decisively and proactively.

Now, let's go back to the trader we discussed at the beginning of this chapter—Alexander. Alexander learned that there is value in reviewing retrospectively what ought to have been done differently, if anything, and then deciding how to adjust to the same kinds of events going forward. He also learned that even when he can't control the symptoms of stress, he can determine whether to stick with his strategy, handle the risk, and reduce the possibility of loss while the stocks are dropping and the market seems unresponsive to positive news. Then he can begin to ramp up when the stocks have started to turn upward and his original thesis looks like it will play out.

Like Alexander, you can change the way in which your trades evolve. You can do this by realizing that you are not your thoughts and fears. You don't need to exert energy trying to cover these feelings. Rather, the only thing you need to do is to recognize your thoughts and feelings and allow them to pass. In the next chapter, we discuss how you can learn to ride out the discomfort associated with stress and begin to trade independently of the negative behavior patterns created as a result.

# CHAPTER 4

# How Fear Inhibits Mastery

## Can You Learn to Lessen the Central Emotion of Fear?

*H*aruki had a bad habit of getting out of winning trades too soon. He had an overwhelming desire to take his profits. For example, not long ago he had one stock in which he made a fair profit, but after he got out it went up another 30 points. He also waited too long before he put on a trade. He might have a conviction level of 80 percent and still not put on the trade. This caused him to lose a lot of upside potential as well. The problem was that Haruki was a perfectionist. He constantly wanted to do more work on a stock before placing the trade. Once he finally made the trade, he quickly pulled out after making a little profit. He was afraid to stay in too long; he was afraid to lose or be wrong.

When I talked with Haruki about his problem, I made a few suggestions. Since he was such an introspective guy, I suggested that he would learn a lot from keeping a diary of his own thoughts so that he could grasp when some random thought or feeling of not knowing enough sidetracked him from getting in or staying in positions. If he could not withstand the urge to withdraw from a winning trade, he could always take the profit and then reenter the trade if his thesis was still intact. While he might not make as much this way, he would still be increasing his profit potential and learning to overcome his fear of failure.

Is it possible to be both fearful and masterful? Given that I have already stated that fear is a natural and inevitable part of the trading game, the answer is yes—but you must learn how to master the fear before you can master the trading game.

Fear is an intense and widely felt emotion among traders. In this chapter, I address the general issue of fear, the underlying roots of fear, and steps that you can take to avoid being under its dominion. In addition, I profile traders and their individual experiences with fear. By reading their stories, I hope that you will be able to relate to their feelings and how those feelings affect trading decisions. Most important, I hope you will see how they—and you—can learn from fear-based mistakes.

## RESPONDING TO FEAR

There are plenty of reasons to be afraid when trading. Traders are, of course, most naturally afraid of losing. Interestingly enough, they may also be afraid of winning too big. Some traders are afraid of uncertainty itself. Others are afraid of the way in which their performance reflects upon their image. Many traders are afraid of disappointment or of disappointing others. And some are just simply afraid of trying.

As fear builds up inside you, it can lead to increasing mistakes—including tendencies toward gambling, paralysis, staying in losing trades, or getting out of winning trades too early.

For example, Leonard was insecure and playing very small. He didn't have an edge or any good ideas. When the market was rallying, he once again allowed the room to spook him out of his long ideas.

"I should have trusted my instincts and stayed with my long positions, instead of getting so much smaller," he said.

Like most fearful traders, Leonard had a problem staying in winners and getting out of losers. It is important to reiterate a central tenet here: Many traders are willing to risk more in a losing trade than they are willing to risk in a winning trade. Because they remember the pain of losing, they hold on to losing trades in hopes of avoiding the pain of the inevitable loss. In the end, this causes them to lose more than they would have lost if they had gotten out at a predetermined stop-loss point, adhering to better risk management principles.

Another example of how fear inhibits successful trading involved a trader named Samuel who seemed to be a master of double-talk. He wouldn't buy more in a stock that he liked even when it went from $6 to $3.50, but he admitted that, given his strong beliefs about the stock, he would have bought into the position if he had not already been in it. He even went so far as to admit that he thought it was a 5:1 or 6:1 risk/reward trade. Samuel's risk manager, Michael, felt Samuel was sending a confused message and trying to avoid being wrong.

However, after the two men discussed the issue, Michael began to see that it was a matter of avoidance due to fear. Samuel defended himself by saying that he was concerned about liquidity and the fact that his trading thesis wouldn't be realized until the following year. Michael pointed out quite clearly how Samuel should be getting bigger, since, with a 5:1 or 6:1 risk/reward profile, this was a potential double grand slam trade. He emphasized the good work Simon was doing and how he needed to dig deeper in high-conviction ideas and size them appropriately relative to a $1 billion portfolio.

Samuel had to learn not to be limited by his fears. He was too busy thinking about daily marking of his positions to the market price rather than P&L targets. He needed to understand that a few good huge ideas with high conviction are actually preferable to a lot of smaller ideas.

Of course, while fear should not guide your trading decisions, it can also not be ignored. In fact, fear should be like an indicator light on your car. When the light comes on, you don't necessarily stop where you are, but you definitely don't ignore it, either. It is a warning that something needs your attention. So is fear. When you are afraid, it is time learn how to "check under the hood." By discovering the source of your fear, you can often rise above it, learning how to use your concerns and the fear of others to your advantage. But your first task should be preventive.

Mechanics know that if you take care of regular maintenance issues, those warning lights won't come on nearly as often. The same applies to traders. By taking a few preventive measures, your fears won't occur as frequently or as severely, and when they do you will know to pay attention.

## DISCIPLINING FOR SUCCESS

You know the cliché: The best offense is a good defense. The same applies to trading. A good trading offense begins with discipline. The markets are unpredictable, the future is uncertain, and most traders feel unsure about themselves and their trading decisions at some time or other. Some traders even feel uncertain most of the time, making it particularly difficult to maintain the requisite discipline throughout the trading period.

To have discipline starts with a plan of action. The more structure that traders can impose on the unstructured nature of the markets, the more likely it is that they will be able to handle the anxieties triggered by the challenges of trading.

Roberto has never developed a disciplined trading strategy. Rather than confront the matter, he simply would accept whatever the market would give him. At times he pressed his bet only to find that the market reversed on him. He was trading scared. Roberto was afraid that if he got out of positions after they reached certain targets that he would miss the big upside moves that he was anticipating—and indeed, this happened on occasion. He had never contemplated setting an independent profit target to use as a lens for making decisions. After we talked, Roberto recognized that if he had done so, he would have lost less money in the past. He is now trying to learn the value of adhering to specific targets in order to increase the efficacy of risk management and to reduce losses.

While the markets may be full of confusion, a trader's decisions do not have to be relegated to instinctive, anxiety-ridden reactions. When a trader defines a target profit, outlines entry and exit points, and designs an overall trading strategy, he has a plan to follow—thus helping eliminate some of the uncertainty in regard to his own actions.

Let's look at some steps taken by Alexander, the portfolio manager I introduced in Chapter 3. It was the middle of November, and he wasn't doing too badly. But he just couldn't seem to break through the $10 million mark. He was afraid to put on size, even when he had conviction. He made close to $4 million the previous month, but would have made $10 million if he had sized his positions in terms of his plan. The real issue: Alexander was afraid to lose money. Even when he had high conviction, he bet small and quickly took his profits, leaving money on the table as well.

My suggestion to him was that he start doing some relaxation exercises and continue to run the same run rate that he had been reaching over the past several months ($1 million to $2 million a month) and that he not press too hard. I reminded him that at the start of the next year, he could create a new objective and a new strategy consistent with bigger goals. He could then increase the size of his trades in incremental fashion. As he did this, he would learn to ride out some of his own discomfort, especially when, deep down, he was certain about his selections. By maintaining his disciplined approach, he was eventually able to stay profitable and avoid potential losses or setbacks that could have followed him into the next year.

John was another trader who didn't stay disciplined. He was basically flat for the year. He had been down $300,000 in the first two months of trading and had then came back masterfully—playing small and in a risk-managed way. But then John became scared that he wasn't contributing enough and started to trade in bigger size with greater volatility. He held on to his losers and took his profits in his winners too fast. I talked with John about the value of sticking to the basics—in this case trading smaller amounts more consistently. In this way he would become profitable even if the amounts were smaller. After a period of continued success with smaller numbers, he could always increase gradually.

Challenging conditions do not require that you give up. But you may have to lower your expectations and set smaller concrete targets. By setting and following a strategy—the most basic of which includes minimizing losses and maximizing winners—traders can avoid the trap of increasing losses in the face of fear.

Of course, discipline is not the same as rigidity. While traders must not change their strategy in a panic, they do need to consider adjustments when there are relevant changes within the markets (such as informational changes, unexpected events, and the like). They also need to constantly look for new ways to assess situations in seeking investment opportunities.

## RELINQUISHING THE NEED TO BE PERFECT

If you take a closer look at fear, you will see that some of it relates to perfectionism. Traders, like many other people, tend to believe that in order to be successful they must be perfect. Not only is this a false assumption, but it is also a dangerous one. In fact, making mistakes helps us learn our most valuable lessons. And since some amount of failure is inevitable anyway, traders are setting themselves up for emotional disaster by expecting perfection in the trading realm.

Often traders who have perfectionist-type traits believe they are being cautious or are simply doing the work needed to make an accurate and successful trade. But the truth is they are covering up a fear of failure, of getting it wrong.

Jamie was an analyst who demonstrated a need to be appreciated; therefore, he desired to play perfectly in order to acquire his sense of value. This was evident when he recommended reducing the size of a position on which he claimed to have a high conviction. This cautiousness reflected Jamie's reluctance to lose money even when the negative data point had not really changed his underlying thesis. After a discussion with Jamie, I pointed out the need for him to separate his own anxieties about P&L from his analyses of the companies he was working on and to make objective recommendations. I also suggested that he consciously try to dig deeper on ideas and start making an effort to get into more dialogues with other analysts in the firm in order to generate more ideas.

Perfectionists like Jamie waste precious energy worrying about the negative consequences of failing. While the worrier concentrates on the mistakes of the past, the perfectionist spends equally valuable time considering the possibility of future failures. These constant thoughts of failure and how to react in case of failure are distracting and obscure the trader's vision of the truth. It is as if the trader is looking at the market through a scratched lens. No matter where he looks or for how long he looks, there will always be a flaw in the picture.

Andy was another perfectionistic trader. Andy was risk-averse and tended to want to be perfect in terms of the development of his systems. While he had big plans to get all his trades on an automated platform, statistical arbitrage, mean-reversion model—which he intended to ramp up with a momentum software model in the second quarter and to double up by the third quarter—the fact was that his constant retooling became a distraction. Andy also demonstrated a problem about giving up control and hiring others to help him leverage his ideas. Again, his risk aversion kept him from hiring people unless he was absolutely certain he could pay for them, and he never seemed to get to that point.

I suggested that Andy build in some specific criteria to give him the confidence to adhere to his strategy at those junctures where his psychological predilections got in the way of his trading. I also suggested that he map out his band of volatility so that when the trades started stretching toward their extremes he could hang in longer within the range of his specified risk tolerances, rather than giving in to his perfectionist traits, getting distracted, and getting out of the game. We also discussed delegating some implementation functions to other traders in order to avoid getting stuck in trading his system.

Jordan, another perfectionist, was so afraid of being wrong that he lacked enough confidence to give his own opinion. He had a compulsive need to present all the information and then to leave the conclusions to someone else. He was on a never-ending hunt for perfect insight and as such never demonstrated any clarity about his views.

And then there was Subash. He was so afraid of being wrong that he was constantly jumping out of positions before the events. He allowed his fear of failure, combined with his desire to make the perfect move, to control his trading decisions to such a degree that he recently recommended covering three-quarters of a position before it went down two points the next day. His tendencies led him into a slump in which his negative framework was causing him much distress, not to mention financial loss.

While every trader should want and aim to do his very best, seeking perfection is not the same. An obsession like this will only hold you back. Many traders are more likely to fail because they hold on to their losers. Perfectionists fail because they don't want to admit their own failures. Listen as this trader describes his experience with a partner.

"Tim has had a bad year, and he is down 10 percent. He has been applying some of his old methodologies to something sensitive to the market. He has a method. He continues to apply that. I apply the same method, but when I see it doesn't work, I stop using it. Tim is holding on to a belief system that may have expired, not just holding on to the losers."

In order to trade effortlessly, masterfully, and in the zone, you have to accept your own imperfection. By understanding, and even admitting, that you are not flawless, you release yourself from the fear of making mistakes. By accepting your mistakes as part of your humanity, you provide yourself with an opportunity to learn from them. I'll go into more depth about perfectionism in Chapter 9. My takeaway point here is that this type of reactive trading is a demonstration of a trader's desire to be right. But masterful traders must not solely consider how often they are right. They also have to consider how much profit they make when they are right versus how much they lose when they are wrong. They have to learn from their mistakes without becoming engrossed in the past, and they have to rely on their trading discipline and psychological energy to help them not trade reactively based on their emotions. Master traders trade big when they have an edge and are never limited by excessive considerations about their P&L balance or cushion or how much they have already made.

## MAINTAINING PSYCHOLOGICAL ENERGY

Fear and success can coexist in traders who have learned the art of discipline in their lives. They can maintain that discipline by defining and adhering to a trading strategy and also maintaining a reservoir of psychological energy. This psychological energy will be a key component in helping them to trade consistently and profitably.

While some traders want to ignore their feelings altogether, lasting success actually requires that traders learn how to stand apart from their emotions and make decisions based on what they know rather than what they feel. Although it is of little value to put on a happy face when you are feeling scared and frustrated, it is of even less value to give in to those destructive feelings and allow them to dictate your trading decisions. Don't deny your feelings, but don't make decisions on the basis of your feelings, either.

### Case Study in the Stress of Losing

Perhaps the most stressful time a trader can face is during a loss. The physical and emotional energy required to deal with a loss can be overwhelming and debilitating. Listen as this trader learns how to maintain psychological energy and recover after a loss.

**Kiev:** When you lose, is that psychologically debilitating?
**Tony:** Absolutely!
**K:** What is the effect?
**T:** You think you are stupid. I just need to prove to myself that I am not dumb, cut my losses, relax, and get back involved. I got

it wrong. Now I need to erase that psychologically and look for the winner.

**K:**     When you're losing, do you also lose your confidence?

**T:**     Yes. That's why getting that one win under your belt is really important. As a psychological tool, every morning when I wake up I say, "I can make money." I get myself into a winning mode. It's kind of what a ski racer does. He memorizes the course.

**K:**     What if you visualized the success? What if you went back to your most successful trades and replayed those and then came in with that winning mind-set?

**T:**     That is probably a good idea.

**K:**     When you are winning, you are more nimble, more flexible. You aren't thinking with a losing mind-set. You are moving forward. That's the mind-set you want to be in, and you don't want to be in it serendipitously. You want to be there with a plan. You can get back into that place after a loss. You can re-create it so that you remember where you were. And even if you've never been there, if you have never felt the exhilaration of winning big, you can imagine it.

**T:**     I was there and made a lot of money.

**K:**     What if you get into that mind-set and begin trading from that place?

**T:**     I will try that.

I recommended this same technique to another trader named Ben, who had had a volatile year. He had been up $4 million, down $8 million, then up $20 million, and then back to flat. He had gotten taken out of his game and had become defensive, in part because of his concerns about credibility and wanting to protect his winnings. He had stopped trading the way he had in the past.

We talked about past successful trades, and he remembered an especially successful experience the previous December. He made $40 million in one month and was really in the zone. As he talked about it, he began experiencing the same sense of calmness that he did when he was trading this way. In this state of mind, he could see everything very clearly while those around him were torn by their own emotions and the confusion in the markets.

"This is the state of mind you want to enter into each morning when you come in to trade," I told him. "By reexperiencing the zone, you can re-create the state of mind that will most enhance your trading. This ought to be the state of mind you get into as you prepare your trading plan for the day."

This state of mind, more than anything else, will enhance a trader's capacity to stay in the zone and to keep trading to win, as opposed to getting fearful, defensive, and subjected to the influences of groupthink—which are a natural response to the uncertainty of the markets.

Ben took my advice and began spending 10 minutes in the parking lot each day visualizing that successful trade before beginning the day's work. He found himself to be, he said, "calmer and more centered."

What happens in the marketplace is a direct result of the emotions and perceptions of the traders themselves. The way in which we understand or misunderstand any given situation and the way in which we react to that information can shape the trades in which we are involved. By learning to start with a winning perspective, traders enhance their ability to handle the fear and uncertainty of the marketplace.

Of course, there is most definitely a mind-body connection to our health. Therefore, traders must understand the importance of their physical well-being in dealing with emotional stresses. In order to combat fear and the depression that often results from it, traders need a healthy lifestyle. For example, most people understand that when they are tired, they are more likely to lose control of their emotions—giving in to depression or allowing their tempers to get the better of them.

Brent has grown to understand this point. We talked about the volatility in the markets and how his emotional reactions were negatively influencing his trades. He needs to apply in trading what he does so well on the tennis court. He cannot allow emotions to interfere with the game. In tennis, he actually uses relaxation exercises between points in order to create the clear mind that allows him to concentrate on the point. So, he is going to start meditation tapes with the hope that he can employ these same techniques while he is trading.

"Trading is stressful," he explained. "You have to work out every day. Physically it's very important, because you get depressed, and then you break down. It happens all the time. The master trader always wants to have a clear and fresh mind for that next month. He doesn't want to be fighting three or four different battles."

Another trader, Dylan, has a good grasp of the importance of both discipline and psychological energy. In his efforts toward mastery, he employs a variety of techniques meeting the needs of both. For example, in an effort to maintain emotional stability, Dylan visualizes on the train ride home at night and again in the morning on the way in to work.

"It is primarily a productivity exercise," he explained. "I visualize myself achieving each of my goals for the day."

In relation to this, he also meditates 20 to 45 minutes each morning and once a week with a group. He considers this the "most important professional tool" that he utilizes. He also keeps a journal.

"I use it as an outlet for my investment ideas," he continued. "Each entry is a couple of sentences about a company or an investment theme. I have strong thoughts daily, and this gets them out of my system."

The journal helps Dylan analyze his ideas to see if there are any patterns and track his emotional tendencies. He also lifts weights twice a week, runs twice a week, and is starting to take up yoga.

While most of these exercises lend themselves to the psychological energy portion of preventive maintenance, Dylan is also keenly aware of the importance of discipline in regard to his trading career. He sets a yearly objective and defines a weekly plan each Friday. He reviews each evening and has developed a contact management system.

"Designing the plan on Friday is my way of creating my future," he explained. "I start with a clean slate and decide what I want to accomplish and how."

## STARTING WITH A CLEAN SLATE

Dylan was onto something big when he said that the likes to "start with a clean slate." Fear often occurs when traders spend time worrying about the past. They ruminate over their past mistakes. They mull over what might have been. They ponder, think, deliberate, reconsider, contemplate, brood, and muse about the what-ifs of their actions. And where does all this lead? Fear. Fear of messing up—again. Fear of looking bad—again. Fear of failing—again.

The masterful trader doesn't waste time and energy worrying about the past. Instead he focuses on the actions that he can take in the here and now—actions that are consistent with his predetermined goal and strategy, actions that will get him involved instead of sitting on the sidelines.

The wise trader learns from his own mistakes (as well as those of others), but he doesn't bed down with them. While there is always value in evaluating what went wrong, what could have been done differently, or what lesson can be learned, there is equal value in getting on with the game. Once you have made your observation, make a note of it so that you won't make the same mistake twice. Then move on.

It is also relevant to understand that not every event has deeply embedded messages to be decoded. Sometimes there is no lesson to be learned except the lesson of hard knocks. Sometimes you may honestly believe that you did everything you could. You prepared every way you knew how, and yet things still didn't work out the way you anticipated. What, then, is the value in worrying over that?

Fear can rob you of your desire to trade and can steal your trading success. Fear, above all other emotions, can paralyze you and leave you impotent in the face of market stress. Success begins by letting go of your fear, concentrating on positive experiences, and working toward your future vision.

# CHAPTER 5

# The Consequences of Negative Emotions

*J*ulian had made some improvements in his trading game—
reducing the number of his positions, becoming more demanding
about the quality of ideas, and not trading stocks just to appease
his brokers. He was also sizing some of his high-conviction ideas, but
he still had a problem with keeping stub ends of trades. He held them
for impending catalysts or because he believed the stock still had some
way to go.

In order to combat the problem, I encouraged Julian to do an analysis
of these trades, to see whether he ought to stay in these positions longer
to increase his P&L or whether he actually lost in these stub ends. Given
the results, Julian realized that when he was holding on to these stub
ends he was acting out of an overreaching ambition. He needed to fully
exit these trades after he took his profits. He also needed to analyze his
statistics in terms of assessing the various strategic reasons for being in
specific trades to ensure there were valid reasons for staying in, even at
small amounts.

Many traders, like Julian, find that negative emotions such as arrogance
and insecurity can lead to a variety of trading errors. When traders give
in to these disturbing feelings and trade on the basis of emotionality
instead of intellect, they often abandon their predetermined strategy—
especially their exit plans. In the heat of trading they may decide that
their strategies are not suited to the situation at hand. They forget
the forethought that went into their plans and the fact that following
an overall strategy tends to lead to more profitable trades in the long

run—maximizing winners and minimizing losers. Under the sway of these negative emotions they often forget that discipline and self-control are the primary routes to success.

The markets are run by fear and greed. Fear, as we have already discussed, leads traders to hold positions (or sell them too soon) in an effort not to lose. Greed, arrogance, and insecurity often result in the same types of errors—holding too long or selling too early—but for different reasons. When traders react to these emotions, they are motivated by an excessive drive for bigger profits. In all four instances (fear, greed, arrogance, and insecurity), it is not the trader's desires (not to lose and to win big) that are in error. The mistakes are a result of using those desires to justify hasty and unwise decisions.

In this chapter I want to look at some of the facets of these negative emotions so as to understand how they manifest themselves in various trading patterns from holding onto stub ends to overreaching and impulsive buying or selling. You will meet a number of traders who battle these impulses as examples of how trading emotionally serves only to take out the processes of rationality, not to actually increase profits.

## GREED AND RISK MANAGEMENT ERRORS

Greed is one of the more overpowering human emotions. It is at times an insatiable desire to be more, do more, and get more. Of course, the key word here is *insatiable*. There is nothing wrong with desiring to do better; greed, however, is the root of a persistent dissatisfaction that leads to more and more effort but never any sense of fulfillment. The end result is often arrogance or insecurity, jealousy, frustration, and impulsive, sometimes even irrational, behavior.

One of the most common ways in which an insatiable appetite for profits manifests itself is in a failure to get out of positions at the right time. Even traders who have set a target and developed a strategy can get caught up in the moment, become invested in the excitement of winning big, and fail to stick to their predetermined plans. While there are obviously times that strategies have to be tweaked, traders need to rely on hard work and sound justification—not an adrenaline rush.

### Case Studies in Getting a Handle on Emotions

Heath typically fails to take his profits when his stocks hit their price targets. Instead, he tries to capture more profit. Then, overcome by conflicting feelings as the stock goes down, he gives back what he has made. His big-profit fever—the chance to make more than he planned—leads him to abandon his original strategy and not take profits when he has them.

The lesson for Heath and others who fail to move their feet on both sides of a trade is to keep close tabs on their profit targets and stop-loss levels for each trade.

Wanting to make more money without thinking about the risk management issues does not make sense. When the desire for profits overcomes a trader's rational approach to assessing ideas and increasing success, that trader is in for trouble.

For example, a mean-reversion trading model works well where you can pick tops and bottoms to reverse direction sooner rather than later. But in a momentum-driven market, this kind of trading too often leads to a tendency to endure a lot of bad trades for too long. Juan is addicted to these. He cannot make himself get out of them, because he is hoping against hope that they will work. He holds on to positions hoping to extract more profit eventually. He does this out of impulsiveness rather than a full understanding of the profit targets.

A while back, Juan gave back half of his year's profits by overstaying his welcome in a couple of huge shorts that kept blowing up in his face. He continued to hold on to them through a short squeeze instead of reducing his exposure and averting disaster. At that point, he hit his stop-out level for having his capital reduced by risk management.

Sometimes traders may unconsciously fall victim to big-profit fever when they demonstrate a reluctance to get out of positions despite the recommendations of the risk manager and management. A trader who does this cannot liberate himself from the urge to succeed. He sticks with his positions even when they are not working for him.

Recently I talked about this with Stuart. As mentioned in Chapter 1, he was very resistant to the idea of being micromanaged by risk management. He believed that his positions were starting to work and that risk management always showed up just when he was starting to make money.

After several discussions, I recommended that he cooperate with risk management and keep his capital usage in line with the capital allocated. He pushed back, arguing that by contract he had greater capital limits and wouldn't accept the reduced limits registered by risk management.

In this sense, an insatiable desire for gain seems to fuel risk-seeking behavior and a reluctance to follow risk management guidelines. How dangerous is this type of behavior? It's dangerous enough for traders to run the added risk of being fired.

Another trader that I spoke with was having trouble with his entry and exit points. His timing was off, and he found that he wasn't maximizing his winners or minimizing his losers. Worse still, he was at a loss about how to get his timing back. In this conversation we discuss his difficulties, and I offer some practical suggestions on how to replace impulsive decisions with rational ones.

**Mitch:** I put a trade on, and the trade starts to work. I am very eager to then take profits. I am so pleased that I am there and making money that I get out.

**Kiev:** So, you miss a big piece of the up move that way? This is quite natural. Traders are often willing to take more risk in losing situations than they are in situations where they have an edge. Your first impulse is to be so thankful that you made a little bit that you get out before things reverse. What makes for mastery is recognizing those patterns and then reviewing your trades so that you have some historical basis for what's happened, to see how much of a move you actually missed. Over time, how much have you missed out on? It may be that you just remember the ones that went up, and you don't remember the ones that went down. It may be that you are doing fine, and if you looked at all the data it's really not that bad, although you may discover that you probably could stay in another point or two.

You may want to consider your entry and exit points. What are the parameters that you're using to govern your decision to get out of the position? For example, do you have a plan in advance to make four points or $100 thousand a day? If you're using that as the criterion, then you can stay in longer because you still have more to go.

**M:** It is difficult to make 4 percent straightaway in a position in three days. So I will be thinking, "I have made so much in a short period of time that I am afraid I may give it back." Then, I cancel out the positive. As a result I tend to miss the second leg of the trade, which really pays off.

**K:** Do you have any kind of rationale behind your targets based on the amount of risk you can take? If you have built a cushion, you've got more capital that you can actually put to work than if you're down. When people are down they sometimes try to make it back rather than reduce their risk. Do you adjust your targets based on how much capital you have at risk? What's your rate of return going to be? Do you have any criteria to use independently of how you feel? Use some of the risk management metrics in order to determine what those numbers are.

**M:** I have a mix of technicals specifically for the target, especially in the chemicals. If there is no trend that the technical can support, I trade smaller amounts. I look at the price and the trading range, and I look for a breakout. I try to have an edge. You have to believe in your edge.

**K:** The critical thing is to ask yourself whether you have done the work to give yourself the conviction that it's a good bet. If you have, then you can keep changing your price target based on additional information, your overall risk profile, and your Sharpe ratio. How much can you afford to risk from a risk management point of view? How much conviction do you have on the basis of your analysis and your understanding of the catalyst? How much do you understand what's going on in the sector? Then you want to have a set of criteria for sizing based on the level of conviction.

**M:** Very often I find the rationale behind the trade is the right one, and my idea is the right one. It's not that the trade doesn't work. What costs me money is that I have been too early on some trades.

**K:** To make a lot of money you want to be early before the rest of the world gets into it. That's not necessarily comfortable, especially with a new idea. The only way you deal with that discomfort is by doing more work, by having more catalysts, more events, more perspective. That will give you the conviction that you need.

**M:** One of the problems is the need to follow a rational investment decision process for our investors. While we may be able to handle not being right all the time, we could have investors walking out of the fund. We have to modify our positions to cut losses, because we can't take a big hit.

**K:** I am not recommending holding on to them. I am talking about the discomfort of the idea. There is never any virtue in building losses to justify that it's going to turn around. It just takes too much work to get it back. So the best risk management is to want to keep the losses down. What's your profit target?

**M:** We start by asking what our investors need. They dictate the goals. Then we have our target, and we work backwards from there.

**K:** I think the first constraint is the investors, and the second is the company's objective. You have to factor in both. You have to find the number that works for you. One way to find it is to look at your track record. What did you do last year? What did you do the year before? Let's say you made 20 percent last year. It would be fair to say this year that you could do 20 percent again. The environment may be a little different. It may make it a little tougher. Are you willing to dig to find the resources within yourself to figure that out? What would you have to do to make 25 percent? As

|       | you said, you need to reverse engineer it. If you are running X amount of money, how big should your positions be? |
|-------|---|

**M:**     That's one of my problems—the right sizing of positions. I realized the sizes of my positions are too small for the ones that work and too big for the ones that don't work. The balance is not quite there. My high-conviction trades have been as high as 18 percent in size. The largest I have now is 12 percent.

**K:**     But when you have a high conviction are you still reluctant to size it?

**M:**     I am very comfortable with some trades, but I still put on too small an amount. I don't necessarily pay the right attention to size. So therefore I basically lose the rewards. Had I sized the trades faster, I would have made more money. Ultimately most of the trades worked.

**K:**     What you really need to do is keep track of your trades. Keep reviewing them and tweaking your methodology. For example, if you had 5 percent positions and they were high conviction, then you would say, "Had they been 10 percent I would have made that much more money." Then set a rule that if it's a high-conviction trade you will start with at least 7 percent. And if you get one more piece of data that supports your view, you could go to 10 percent. You create a blueprint to follow. You don't let your own feelings of comfort or discomfort interfere. Go back over your trades to see where most of your money was made. You are likely to find that most of your money was made in a handful of trades, probably those you consider high-conviction trades, where you pressed the bet. The review may reveal that you didn't make enough of those trades.

   Ask yourself: "Is this starting to work? What more can I do to build my confidence? Who else can I talk to in order to get a handle on it?" Then try to get bigger. At the same time, maybe you have some trades where you have lost because you have gotten too attached to them. You want to be able to identify that pattern.

**M:**     Can you give me three or four things to think about so as to manage these issues?

**K:**     The first thing is to have a target. What's your goal? Do you have a weekly target or a daily target? Let's say you want to make 20 percent for the year. What does that come to on a monthly, weekly, and daily basis? When you come in on a given day, look at your portfolio and consider how you are going to make money on that day. You want to use your goal as a lens by which to see what position(s) you have to make for each day.

**M:**     That's interesting. You are saying that there are some trades where you have short-term catalysts. Then you have other trades that are long core trades, and you just keep on working them to make yourself more comfortable.

**K:** Exactly! You should have some companies that you really know. There are catalysts and announcements, and you want to track all the news related to what's going to change the price. Even in your long-term core positions you can add and trade around it. You want to know a little bit more. The more you know, the more intensity you're going to bring. If you're driven by the goal, by the number, that will help push you through the discomfort that you feel.

**M:** Sometimes that goal puts so much pressure me, it forces me to make a decision to lock in my profits. Sometimes I find it hard to balance the positive and negative of having an objective.

**K:** That's exactly the balance you have to find. You need to be driven by the goal, and then when it makes you uncomfortable you need to learn how to meditate, take a break, deep breathe—things that can help you stay focused on the goal.

**M:** Not be paralyzed by it.

**K:** The best trader is focused. She is centered and calm. She is not trying to win. She is not winning because she is great. She has learned how to be comfortable with intensity. You have to learn how to ride with it. If you just made some profit, and it's working, then stay with it. You are getting too anxious, so you are getting out and are missing the bigger opportunity. Learning to monitor your own responses is a very critical part of this. This is more psychological than it is analytical. The excitement of having made it and the thought of not making it are awful. You have to let those go. I think these are important considerations. You frame it and then learn to manage.

**M:** How do you deal with something that doesn't work? Do you just leave it for the day, think about it, and come in the next morning?

**K:** Again, use the P&L as your guide. You don't want to be trapped by your inclination to be a contrarian. If it's not working, you should consider that maybe somebody in the world knows something that you don't know. You want to be invested only in making money, not in an idea. You can tolerate the discomfort in terms of having an idea that is not yet accepted, but there is no virtue in taking a lot of pain for no reason. You want to think more in terms of using your contrarian view to help you find ideas, not necessarily manage the portfolio. Your Sharpe ratio is a very valuable statistic. If you have a Sharpe ratio of less than one, then maybe you shouldn't be taking more risk, but if you have two or three or better, then you could be taking more.

Your Sharpe ratio will give you an idea of how good your risk management is. What's the ratio of your wins over your losses? Are you making more money in your wins than you are losing in your losses? If you are, that's good and that's further justification for getting bigger.

**M:**    I see what you're saying. Actually I think that's the key problem.

**K:**    It could be an impressive batting average but not an impressive slugging average.

**M:**    Actually, my P&L has started picking back up again.

**K:**    Every day you should go through your positions and consider if you should be in each one. Then ask yourself if you are big enough.

**M:**    Eighty percent of my ideas worked, but either the timing was too early or the size was too small. I could have 70 percent of my trades winning. The size of my winning trades was too small versus the size of two losing trades. So it was all canceled out.

**K:**    First, you need to work on size. Second, you need to work on the long hold. You need to use the statistics from risk management to help you size your trades. You want to get a holding period analysis—looking at your trades over a one-day period, six days, two weeks, three weeks, four weeks, and more. You want to find out where you make your money in terms of holding period. The more you understand the way in which you trade, the more you can tweak it. If you just trade but don't know what the underlying profile is, you don't know whether you have to adjust.

This conversation told me that Mitch was operating from instinct without analyzing either the size of his positions or the level of his convictions. What I advised—by telling him to keep a journal and other suggestions—was that he needed to ground himself. He needed to step back a bit, notice when his emotions were getting the best of him, and to operate apart from those emotions, all the while learning to exist in the gap between where he was and where he wanted to be, however uncomfortable he might be.

## THE DIFFERENCE BETWEEN CONFIDENCE AND ARROGANCE

In a world that is consumed with self-esteem issues, one may wonder what could possibly be wrong with a little confidence. Nothing is wrong with a *little* confidence. In fact, traders need to be confident in their work. They need to develop the skills to dig deeply and gain the information required to make successful trades. But a little confidence based on a solid foundation of work is a lot different from arrogance based on an inflated sense of one's self.

Emilio was doing reasonably well in buying gas company stocks during dips and selling them when they moved up in 2002. However, as things tended to run smoothly he began to develop a problem with overconfidence. As a position would begin to do well, he would assume (without justification) that things were going to continue moving upward. Instead of taking his profit when the price reached his target, he started holding on and then began giving up his profits as things came tumbling down.

I talked with him about this—how it appeared that he was basically changing his strategy in midstream by getting bigger without doing the requisite work. One solution I suggested was that he take his profits, wait for the dips, and then get back into the positions. If, after trying this, he began to find that he was consistently correct, then he could consider increasing the size of his initial positions rather than doing so after the move. Emilio agreed with my assessment, and this became his new strategy.

Another trader, Warren, also hurt himself by being too cocky. He complained that the $5,000 a day he was making consistently wasn't going to add value to his firm, so he wanted to make more. Unfortunately, he went about it the wrong way. Like Emilio, he held on to his positions even after he had a profit in them and gave back much of what he had made. I tried to convince him of the value of building up a track record and gaining true confidence. I explained that after he had established this kind of credibility and financial basis, he could resize his positions and increase his results. Unfortunately, Warren failed to see the value of my suggestion.

Like Warren, any trader who has a false sense of confidence in his abilities is often not open to suggestions. He tends to trade more presumptuously, based more on emotions than on his data and goal. With an exaggerated view of his abilities, he will begin to develop an "I can do no wrong" mentality.

## MISTAKES OF INSECURITY

Many traders privately compare themselves to others. If they are performing better than their counterparts, then they will become arrogant. But if they are performing in a less successful manner, they may be jealous and insecure. Instead of being confident in their abilities, they battle with an imbedded sense of insecurity that directs their efforts and compounds their stress. While insecurity is the opposite of arrogance, both can lead traders to mistakes.

## Case Study in Misapplied Meditation and Visualization Techniques

Dugan is an analyst whose insecurity is leading him to efforts to control his impulse to win with greater profitability. Although he employs the techniques of meditation, visualization, and journaling on a regular basis, he is using them to squelch his insecurity, instead of using the techniques to calm down—to take his emotions out of the equation—so he can get to the root cause of his mistakes.

**Kiev:** Meditation is a useful tool in trying to deal with tension and anxiety. However, I am afraid that you are using it in an attempt to manage your positions or your trading career. Am I reading that correctly?

**Dugan:** I felt I was easily distracted and not as productive in the afternoons. So I use visualization to make my day more productive.

**K:** How do you do it? Do you anticipate what you are going to do? Do you have a kind of template in your mind that you follow?

**D:** Yes. For five to ten minutes on the train going home, I picture myself going through the routine of the next day. I think about the day with an open mind, not getting tense and letting things bother me, just being relaxed and open-minded. Mainly, I just go through my objectives for the day—from when I get into the office until when I leave, most of which is research-related.

**K:** Do you visualize yourself achieving each of your goals in order to get distracting thoughts out of your system?

**D:** No, I have some very strong investment thoughts.

**K:** Do you want to get those out of your system?

**D:** No, not at all. *Express* would be a much better word.

**K:** Do you start with a clean slate on Friday?

**D:** Each Friday I take a blank sheet of paper, and I say, "Okay, this is me creating my life. What are the three things I want to accomplish by next week's end?" The way I use visualization is to picture myself going through my day, achieving my objectives. So when I come in, I am focused.

**K:** The questions are: How much is your activity governed by the ideas? What issues do they generate, and what more is fostered by the ideas? What challenges lead you to do more? Are you focusing on the steering of the machine rather than getting out and examining the road?

**D:** The journal and daily planning enable me to go deeper. Without them, it would be easier to stay at the surface level because I wouldn't be consciously forcing myself to focus.

**K:** Let's consider something else. Where do you stumble? Where do you give up? Where do you not challenge yourself as much as you can? When you discover the answer to those questions, then you should apply the meditation to those issues. You are doing the exercises, but how are you applying them to your trading? Use the processes of meditation and journaling in the service of sizing and gaining conviction and making money.

**D:** Journaling brings out the thoughts inside of me. Writing things down brings things to the surface of my consciousness.

**K:** But have you done all the work you can do to back up the ideas?

**D:** In some cases, but certainly not in all cases.

**K:** You have the idea. You have some data points. The questions are: What do you need to get bigger? What work do you need to increase your level of conviction? I hear what you are doing. But what purpose does your visualization serve? You are doing all these things so you can handle your trading career, but you are not necessarily doing more work to generate more P&L.

**D:** I have a strong feeling. I want to express it on paper. I am going to go back and evaluate. I want to look at these feelings that I have. I want to see whether I am right or wrong, to see if there are any lessons there. Is that the wrong objective of the journal? Are you saying that the objective of the journal is to record my feelings and then to ask myself what else I can do to transform those feelings into P&L today?

**K:** Currently, you are tracking how you feel to see if your feelings have any meaning. This has to do with a kind of self-monitoring.

**D:** That's how I was going to tangibly take it and turn it into P&L over time. At the end of the day it feels good to write my feelings down and express them. As for the logical use of that data, I want to study it and take lessons from it.

**K:** I hear what you are saying.

**D:** But your point is to ask why I don't use these thoughts to generate P&L right now? What else can I do right now?

**K:** If you want to use this as a stimulus to help you understand how you feel and the meaning of your feelings, that's fine. But it can also be more. You can use it to understand where you are holding back. Ask yourself: Where did I have high conviction? Was I big enough? Could I have done more work in the ones that were big bets? What more could I have done by way of studying my ideas so as to have been justified as being bigger? Where was I stopping in terms of what I have done? Is there more work to get it done, or were there reasons why I lost money? Could I have reduced my losses by getting out sooner? What were the reasons why I stayed in those, anyway? Why do I have ideas written down that I never got into?

**D:**   I think that's the key. I have a lot of good ideas that don't make it into the portfolio.

**K:**   This is where visualization can come in, because you have to really face the truth as to why you are not getting these ideas into play. What additional work can you do to get the validation you need to put these ideas into action? I think underneath it all there is a concern that you have about looking good. You don't want to appear foolish in front of your peers or superiors. It's a principle that is running your life. You are writing things down, but you're not doing anything. It's all very subtle. You write something down, and then you say, "Should I? No. I will go and do something else."

**D:**   I am using this as a crutch, aren't I? The fact that I am writing it down is a replacement for actually doing it.

**K:**   You really need to consider how you are holding back.

**D:**   That is what half my journal entries are about.

**K:**   You are afraid to own your ideas, to follow through, to risk a bad reaction from a superior if you are wrong.

**D:**   I want to make sure that I am right. I want to make sure that I do not lack conviction. You see what I am saying? There is obviously a big difference.

**K:**   So, you have an idea that you think is a good one, but you don't have enough data to build the high conviction? Can you do more work?

**D:**   I guess I haven't been that sensitive about it.

**K:**   Are you telling your subordinates to do the work? If so, you have to sell them on doing the work.

**D:**   I want people to be motivated. I want them to have a rewarding experience. I want to develop that connection with them because I understand what I am thinking.

**K:**   Let's think it through. Say you think XYZ is worth putting on. You want a little more information. Do you have somebody you can tell? Can you say, "Listen, call around about XYZ and find out how sales and inventory are doing"? Or do you hesitate? Do you want them to generate their own work?

**D:**   No, I don't hesitate to ask. I think if anything I should probably be taking a couple of minutes to explain why I am asking it.

**K:**    What are your preconceptions about how you want to manage people? Are you trying not to push them too hard? What are you not doing to get the results you need? Do you think that they are too busy to bother with your ideas?

**D:**    There are two things that I can visualize. Number one, I can visualize having a body of research in a certain period of time by a certain deadline. That gives me conviction one way or another. Then I can visualize presenting these ideas and the results that follow—whether it works or not and my reaction to that. That's fascinating, because I have never done that. I think that would be very helpful. In terms of where I am stopping with the junior analysts, I don't know.

**K:**    Let's get back to your goals. You should be driven by the goal, using it as a lens through which to see what work needs to be done, which position needs to be sized. To reach that target you have to say, "Okay, I have to do this much work, make this many more calls, do this much more digging." You have to figure out if you can do it or if you need to delegate it, but you have to get it done. You have to get past your resistance in order to make X amount of dollars in XYZ or in retail stocks. That's what visualization should be about. You are doing the visualization, and you feel like you are in the zone, but you're not putting it into action.

**D:**    It's something that we have never done. I particularly have been thinking much more in that process of starting with an end goal and then working backwards.

**K:**    It is useful to pick some number. Pick the number you made last year. The purpose of the number or the target is to use it as a motivator or driver of this process.

**D:**    At the end of the day we have a goal, and we need to do what it takes to reach it.

**K:**    That will help move you in the right direction, because you will be much more target-oriented. Ask yourself what work needs to be done and who needs to do it.

**D:**    So, what's holding me back? I think there are three things. The stocks are up a lot, a lot of my very smart friends are shorting the stocks, and it's not an area that my trader knows at all. In a sense, all three of these things are completely irrelevant. These three factors have probably slowed me down a bit. The reality is that I may have a 15 percent position but we're at zero.

**K:**    What's the risk/reward?

**D:**    I haven't worked it out exactly. I am guessing two to one. That's a key question.

**K:** If it's two to one, it certainly could be at least a 2 or 4 percent position. You are hesitating because your trader doesn't normally trade these.

**D:** He would say that he has an affinity for a certain type of business. He will just tell me that if I want to do it, to go ahead and do it. It will be on me. But if he doesn't buy it, if he is not really excited about it, I don't want to do it.

**K:** Do the work then. Go in and tell him that you are fired up. Tell him that it's a bonanza. At the end of the day, it's his decision, but you shouldn't short-circuit your own enthusiasm and your own investment.

**D:** But maybe it's not a bonanza. I can articulate it that way, but why even do it if he is not going to want to do it?

**K:** That may be a source of frustration, and that may explain the motivation for some of your meditation. You are having these strong thoughts and meditating and journaling gets them out of your system. It sounds like you are trying to meditate in an effort to calm down and purify yourself so that you don't get too frustrated.

**D:** I think you are right. The key is that my efforts are not getting rid of the creative ideas. They are getting rid of the frustration of not having great ideas in the portfolio.

**K:** The whole idea is to figure out how to express your vision, not how to squelch it. You have to figure out how to do that within your environment. You have to believe in your ideas and present them. You may also want to create a spreadsheet on all your ideas. Mark if they are presented, if they are accepted, and how they did regardless. Go back in a few months and look at how many of your ideas were successful and of those how many made it into your portfolio.

**D:** My trader will accept everything I present to him.

**K:** Then why are you hesitating? It has to be something you learned early in your life where you are avoiding a negative response.

**D:** I am not pushing the envelope.

**K:** Are you afraid to be told no? Are you afraid to have your idea rejected, afraid it won't make money?

**D:** Maybe. I know it's going to be uncomfortable.

**K:** That's good. You know that you are stretching when you are uncomfortable. The day it becomes comfortable, you should find something else. You're going to grow only when you are stretching.

**D:** When I have a super idea, I have no problem going in, being very strong, saying that we need to be bigger. But I think there is a

K:   level below that where my conviction is not super strong, but I still have some really good ideas. Maybe I haven't done all the work, but enough work has been done. It's a good enough idea. It could be a great idea. That's where from time to time I am falling short.

K:   Do you see where all this ties in? You can use visualization in the service of presenting your leads in a more powerful way. It is fine to use it to help deal with your frustration. But it will be even more productive to use visualization as a means of helping you do what is necessary to avoid stifling yourself by virtue of not speaking up and testing the limits. You have to get past your own baggage. Hopefully, your desire to succeed can fire you up and help you get past these obstacles.

This discussion underscores the importance of learning to be proactive and not limited by self-concerns. Instead of worrying about what needs to be done to make one look better or to avoid making oneself look worse, traders should be channeling their energy into making a profit. The best traders learn how to set aside their arrogance or insecurities and let the work they have done and the choices they have made guide their decisions. Regardless of whether they appear arrogant or insecure, traders often develop dissatisfaction with small wins. They waste precious energy trying to imitate the superficial moves of other traders. In other words, they don't truly investigate the differences between themselves and a masterful trader. They simply want to find the quick fix that will enable them to reach the same levels of profit. Of course, steps like these are more likely to lead to increased failure and insecurity than to success.

## Case Study on Insecurity

Glenn provides a good example of how several negative emotions can become entangled in the psychological makeup of a trader and impinge on his trading experiences. At a recent management meeting the question arose as to whether he should receive a portion of the management fee rather than just a percentage. This would involve more responsibilities on his part in exchange for the recognition and the economics. The question becomes more complicated when one considers Glenn's personality.

Glenn constantly searches for recognition—a repeated behavior pattern fostered from childhood by parents who still fail to give him the recognition he seeks. He has a built-in insecurity that manifests itself as an unhealthy self-interest and an unquenchable desire for more recognition. As Glenn receives recognition, he develops more of an inflated sense of himself and slacks off in his efforts. This egotism drives him to constantly seek more affirmation but to coincidentally reduce his efforts. In fact, past experience suggests that given this promotion, Glenn's performance would change little, but his desire for more recognition would increase.

Whether battling arrogance or insecurity, such a trader is often consumed not only with his financial success but also with how other traders view his abilities. Remember, greed is not limited to a desire for money alone. It includes the desire for power and prestige, a desire that can affect a trader's ability to think clearly in a number of ways.

For example, Daniel was concerned about connecting with other traders. He seemed to demonstrate a need to win approval. This preoccupation was distracting him from vetting ideas in the best possible way and organizing his data flow. Although he claimed to have leadership skills, he was actually more focused on his own approval ratings than leading or building a team of supportive people around him.

To trade profitably requires controlled aggressiveness rather than compulsion. Traders who fail to control their impulses are setting themselves up for heavy losses.

I explored with Daniel ways in which he could increase his confidence—among them tracking how many of the recommendations based on his analysts' ideas are hits versus the ones not recommended so as to see what his batting average is. I also suggested that he learn to differentiate among the trading event, his emotional reactions to it, his interpretation of the event, and his response in moments of reactivity. When these things are clearly outlined on paper, he can learn to be more objective about his responses, trade more in terms of his goal-directed strategic objectives, and spend less time trying to look the part of a heavy hitter.

To overcome these sabotaging emotions, traders must go back to following a goal-directed daily strategy. The value of a goal is that it gives traders a reason for getting out of the trade. The daily target gives traders a tangible reason to let go of those unnecessary risks and to channel negative impulses toward the positive desire of reaching a predetermined target.

## WHY NOT TO AVOID NEGATIVE FEELINGS

Some people waste a great deal of time trying to deny or suppress their bad emotions. It doesn't work. A more useful solution is to open up, let your defenses down, and allow yourself to get in touch with negative feelings. They are not likely to disappear, but you can lessen their impact. Rather than have them percolate below the surface, acknowledge these negative feelings while giving yourself the time and the space to let them float away.

Letting go of destructive emotions means being honest about their existence while you are leaving them behind you. You can improve, get bigger, set higher goals, and achieve those goals; along the way, you'll be depriving those negative feelings of oxygen.

Out-of-control feelings can still surface, but all you need to do is recognize your discomfort when they arise, rather than halt your progress. In some cases, traders use negative emotions as an excuse not to "go for the gold." Have you ever admonished yourself by saying, "I shouldn't be so greedy" or "I can't do this because I'll look arrogant"? These are all part of the same impulse. You're so busy avoiding certain feelings that you don't make an honest effort to achieve your objectives. What happens is that you're trying to mask a lack of effort as not wanting to appear arrogant. When traders seek to avoid negative emotions entirely, they only create a different set of emotions and a different set of problems.

## Case Study on Avoidance

Such was the case with Will. He was well on the way to reaching his $200 million but then became too cautious after an unusually big win of $60 million. He failed to get as big in some other potentially big ideas and was too small in several positions. Rather than being pleased, Will said that making a huge amount of money in one trade was "surreal" to him. He decided that he didn't want to be "too greedy" and didn't apply himself as intensively at that time as he now believes he should have. After our discussion, Will agreed that he had learned from the experience and in the future he would pay more attention to his emotional response to success. He would also make a greater effort to stay focused on his target and not get sidetracked by major wins or losses—or by the feelings of exuberance or despair that such wins or losses trigger.

Traders need to first of all acknowledge that negative emotions are going to creep up at some point in time. They are normal reactions to the various stresses that a trader experiences every day. Because they are normal, it's counterproductive to work too hard to avoid such feelings. Notice them, but don't dwell on them. They are beside the point. Keep heading in the direction you chose and those emotions will soon be irrelevant.

A master trader has a very sensible approach to handling outsized opportunities. He runs a very risk-managed strategy. When he is down, he gets into cash and waits for opportunities. He takes no extraordinary bets. He is not distracted by the success of others. He is confident and knows that eventually his opportunity will appear, and he plans to be ready for it. He shows a measured awareness of the dangers of wanting huge profits and excessive risk taking, but at the same time he is willing to call a spade a spade and deal as realistically with events as possible. Meanwhile, he continues to do his work and look for evidence to support his developing thesis.

## HOW NEGATIVE EMOTIONS LEAD TO IMPULSIVE BEHAVIOR

When traders fail to acknowledge and learn from their negative emotions, they begin to make decisions based not just on what they think or know but also on how they feel. They forget their discipline and trade according to momentary, spontaneous impulses that they later regret.

Nelson lost two points in an oil service company that was going down. A couple of calls he received before entering the stock convinced him it would go up. In retrospect, Nelson said that he shouldn't have traded something he didn't know personally based on a couple of calls about debt forgiveness in a stock that was going down on the tape.

Skip had a different excuse. He claimed that when he got bigger recently it was the wrong time. It was just when his stocks were starting to drop, and he was pushing to size things instead of sticking with his conviction levels.

Then there are traders like Ambrose. He had no specific plan or strategy and only an anemic sense of what it would take to put up better numbers in the coming year than he put up the previous year. He traded a great number of sectors, far more than anyone would be able to follow, and lost money in banks, which presumably was the sector about which he knew the most. He had no rationale about sizing his positions and building a portfolio based on the potential in the sectors he was trading. When asked about his problems, he simply argued that he "was opportunistic."

Relying on instinct rather than discipline, going for the opportunistic gain rather than the high-conviction gain—all such moves are the results of impulsive reactions, and you can pay dearly for them. Most people are, in fact, willing to take more risk when facing loss than they would when facing gain. For example, a trader who is in a winning trade is more likely to take his profits too quickly and get out, whereas a trader who is in a losing trade, according to theory, is more likely to invest more or at the least stay in longer, in hopes that the trade will come around and that he will make back his losses plus some. As illogical as it sounds, it is true. And most traders know it's true, because they have experienced it themselves.

The very fact that traders abandon reason to take more risk when losing gives credence to our impulsive nature. Humans are bent on acting according to their inspirations. Unfortunately for traders, those inspirations are often wrong. Whenever a trader reacts, whether in a winning trade or in a losing trade, and makes a sudden move outside his original strategy without serious forethought, his decision can be classified as impulsive. In some cases there will be a measure of success, but in the long run impulsiveness is a great danger to traders because it relieves them of their discipline.

Have you ever been on a long drive and decided to take a shortcut—not a shortcut that you know, but a line on a map jutting off from the highway, one that you estimate will shave about 20 minutes from your trip? Have you ever taken that shortcut only to find out that the hills, curves, and potholes in the road actually wound up lengthening your trip instead of reducing it? That's what happens when traders allow themselves to concentrate on the goal more than the strategy to achieve the goal.

They are lured by what seems to be a shortcut, an easier, quicker, more painless path. They have their eyes on the final destination instead of the road in front of them.

"What?" you say. "I thought the goal was important, essential, a necessity to becoming a trading master."

But therein is the misconception. It is not the goal itself that is so important. It is the process of working toward a goal. Successful traders believe that if they do everything necessary in pursuit of the vision, the vision will take care of itself. As I mentioned before, the law of probability indicates that even bad decisions will sometimes lead to favorable outcomes, and sometimes good decisions will lead to bad outcomes. But masterful traders know that if they follow their plan consistently they are more likely to achieve success.

What can you do to steer clear of impulsive decision making that results from negative emotions? The answer to that question begins by understanding the biggest snares. Let's discuss a few of them here.

## "Everybody's Doing It"

Some refer to it as following the herd or groupthink. It's similar to the peer pressure we hear so much about in our younger years. Unfortunately, adults, too, fall prey to the "if everyone's doing it so must I" mentality. Afraid to miss out on something that everyone else is getting excited about, traders often jump into trades based solely on two bits of information or what their buddies are doing. Because everyone has a natural desire to be accepted, traders, too, battle the urge to go with the flow. This can lead them to choose to be with the wrong majority instead of the right minority.

Monty was a trader who seemed to make his trades based on what he was hearing from hedge fund cohorts. He never really had his own perspective or did his own technicals. His oil company ideas weren't compatible with the oil team's ideas but were lined up relative to chemicals, energy, industrials, and other stocks. It wasn't any surprise when his profitability took a plunge.

## Imitation Is Not Always Flattering

Although there are some basic concepts among all master traders, there are a lot more aspects of mastery that must be hammered out individually. Each trader is unique. He has different strengths and weaknesses, skills and knowledge, fears and breaking points. Therefore, what works for one trader does not always work for another. Unfortunately, traders sometimes forget that simple fact. Seeing the success of a counterpart, they may try to imitate his actions.

Bentley saw Nelson making money in relative value plays and tried to emulate him. This effort caused him to act more like a portfolio manager over a period of four months. During that time he was basically hedged and holding on to things that were going against him or hedging them out with other positions and ending up being stuck with bigger losses than in the past. In his effort to imitate Nelson he had gotten way off course and out of his own style of trading, to which I persuaded him to return in an effort to regain regular profitability.

Once he was back trading his old style, he began to feel a lot more empowered. When asked why he had gotten so far off course, he said that he had thought everything in the firm was changing and that he ought to change as well. I suggested that his basic trading style was far more hard-wired than he had thought, and that change meant tweaking his style and expanding on it, not radically altering it based on an imitation of another trader's moves.

Rarely do traders like Bentley recognize all of the behind-the-scenes effort that has taken place in order for another trader to achieve his measure of success, and rarely do they recognize how ingrained their own styles are. While imitating certain masterful concepts is beneficial, impulsively imitating specific actions is not.

## Justifying Your Answers

Sometimes traders who faced the pain of impulsive decisions that have gone bad go on to commit the same mistake again … and again … and again. While others in the firm (especially their risk managers) can see a pattern developing, they seem oblivious. The traders around them wonder how they could be so blind to their own mistakes. But the answer is actually very simple. Each time they make an impulsive decision, they find sufficient justification to convince themselves that this trade will be different.

Regardless of who they are or what their profession is, once individuals make a decision they tend to look for information to confirm that the decision is right and to deny any information indicating that their choice is wrong. This type of prejudicial work is detrimental, because traders are not getting the clear picture.

It is for this reason that traders who are acting irrationally can say, even when facing a pattern of losses, "What happened? Everything seemed to indicate that I was right on the money."

Research shows that traders even seem to reprogram their memories in order to justify their actions after the act. It is for this reason that I constantly recommend that traders keep a trading journal. By writing down your thoughts, actions, and feelings while they are happening you will have an accurate reflection of the facts of the event as it actually took place—not another interpretation of your emotional reactivity.

## Failing to Set a Goal

Earlier I discussed how some traders place all their energy on the outcome. There are also traders who take the other extreme—placing too little emphasis on a goal.

While it is imperative to focus on the strategy to reach a goal, it is impossible to do that if you never set one in the first place. And for various reasons, many traders are reluctant to do just that.

Perhaps it is a fear of failing: If you never set a goal, you can never feel the pain of not meeting it. Or perhaps it is an aversion to commitment. The point is, if you don't have a goal to work toward, your trading behavior will most likely be erratic and unpredictable.

For example, Kamal complained about the market uncertainty and felt burned out. But he resisted the idea of setting a goal. Instead, he said, his objective was "to make as much money as possible." But Kamal believed he did this only when he had high conviction. He wanted to trade using a seat-of-the-pants approach rather than more systematically. What he didn't realize was that by establishing a goal and trading with a more conscious effort, he could be using more capital and making more money.

Another trader, Carey, had an elaborate system for tracking his trades historically. He kept careful notes about what he was doing right and wrong. He hoped for six big trades a year when he would produce 3 percent profits on his whole portfolio. Meanwhile, he was looking to trade daily but had not yet gotten the idea of committing to specific targets. It all depended on "what the market will give me," he said, and the market had been choppy of late. Carey did not yet understand that by not setting a goal he was contributing to an impulsive trading style that could not take advantage of the opportunities that are out there.

Traders who fail to set a goal may live for the thrills associated with winning big but will likely experience the agony of defeat more often.

*   *   *

So, what can traders to do in order to avoid these psychological traps? First, they need to be realistic about their abilities. As I discuss in more detail later in Chapter 13, traders need to set goals that are neither too easy nor too difficult to reach. Beyond simply setting a goal, consideration must be given to establishing a vision that is both reachable and challenging at the same time. When traders set too high a target, they quickly become discouraged and begin trading out of emotional reactions in an attempt to get the quick fix.

Second, traders need to think about their assumptions. Assuming the market is always the factor in a loss is not being honest. Assuming that your co-workers always know what's best is not being smart. Assuming that a goal is not necessary is setting yourself up for failure. Think about your assumptions. Question your own beliefs. Dissect them. Consider how you can think and act more realistically.

Keep in mind that discipline is an important criterion in the pursuit of your vision. However, discipline is not the same as rigidity. It does not negate the need for flexibility. Top traders recognize that the marketplace is in a constant state of ebb and flow and therefore the processes of trading will also need to change and adapt. Adaptation and impulsiveness are not the same. Be flexible enough to make a change based on a valid piece of information that you have carefully considered. As traders increase their tolerance for anxiety, they can become more adaptable and able to trust themselves more readily, to read the markets more accurately, and to react to the unexpected more quickly.

Once again, this points to the importance of how you evaluate the situation. If you stay focused solely on the outcome, you will most likely have a lot of impulsive decisions, poor processes, and some temporarily lucky outcomes but overall failure. However, if you set your goal, establish your strategy, and focus on the process itself, you will most likely have satisfactory results in a consistent manner.

Studies show that people who make spur-of-the-moment decisions are more likely to be wrong. When pressed for time, they tend to use rules of thumb or their own memories to make decisions. When a trader is anxious and trying to make a quick decision, those standards usually point us toward what's comfortable, and what's comfortable is often simply not correct. In addition, anxiety uses up a lot of our psychological energy. Therefore, when time is limited it is hard to seriously consider all the possibilities carefully and objectively. So, impulsive traders can benefit most by simply slowing down.

Look at each decision from a variety of angles. Understand that while the past offers clues, the future is never clearly defined. Do the work. Seek information from a variety of sources. Don't be in a hurry. While some decisions have to be made on the spur of the moment, many do not. If it can wait, then wait until you have given it a little more thought. Rather than acting impulsively, rather than being frightened or profit-hungry, simply stay on course. The more detailed plan of action you have before a trade, the less you will have to worry about reacting on the basis of fear, arrogance, or insecurity.

# CHAPTER 6

# Personalities
# and Stress

**R**yan was an impulsive, intuitive trader. Going with his gut, he experienced at least a modicum of success. However, he struggled with getting too big too fast and often did not do enough work to justify his actions.

Malcolm was a confident trader, despite the fact that he was down $3 million and his performance had been sluggish for about a year. Last year he got off to a huge start and was up $15 million by midyear. Then he gave back $7 million in the latter half of the year. He attributed his poor results to the problems of integrating two new members to his team. Still, Malcolm was doing the work and was confident that his longer-term ideas (which constituted the bulk of his portfolio) were going to work.

Kai was a sucker for a sell-side analyst's story and had a history of getting into long-term positions, believing in the story, and then getting hurt when he couldn't interpret the meaning of selected catalysts. As such, he repeatedly lost money in longer-term ideas driven by fundamentals. He was almost flat for the month after having been down over $1 million. Now he was concentrating on short-term trading and futures and was consciously avoiding long-term trades.

Stuart, though focused and committed, was also down about $1 million. Unfortunately, Stuart's statistics revealed that he was taking too many positions and was earning money only in long-only, long-term positions. He thought that he needed to expand his coverage to small-cap stocks in his space where there might be some good longer-term investment opportunities. His greatest need was to raise his awareness of what constitutes a good short and to manage his risk better.

Each of these traders is unique, just as each human being is unique. Our life experiences and beliefs work with our genes to form a distinctive personality in each one of us. These personalities, in conjunction with our individual strengths, weaknesses, and memories, affect how we react to stress. As such, no two people will react exactly the same way, even if exposed to the same stressful event.

While it is human nature to try to label individuals according to generalized similarities (e.g., nerds, jocks, geeks, macho men), each trader is going to bring his or her unique personality into the trading game and perform and react in ways that are related to his or her individual experiences. For example, someone who has been fearful since early childhood may have a harder time dealing with loss than someone who has experienced much success and confidence in life. Similarly, a trader who is an avid fan of learning and who loves the process of gathering and sorting through new information will most likely enjoy the research aspect of trading more than someone who is known as an impulsive daredevil type.

Given this perspective, it is understandable why it is so hard to give generalized trading advice—especially in the area of how to handle stress. Without knowing you personally, it is hard to predict exactly how you will handle stress or the problems you may encounter in your trading career.

But humans have a wonderful capacity to find aspects of almost any story to which they can identify. Whether watching a movie, reading a book, or listening to a joke, the human brain searches for specific traits similar to its own. That is why in this section I discuss several trading profiles. My hope is that every reader will find some elements of himself or herself in these portraits. When you find yourself saying, "That's the way I feel," or "That sounds like me," or "I relate to that," pay especially close attention. Seriously consider and evaluate how the depiction resembles your own traits. Are you facing similar difficulties as a result of similar personality characteristics? Does the individual handle stress in a familiar way? Can you benefit from the same solutions that the profiled trader used? Would you be willing to try?

Remember, these chapters are not here to give you a step-by-step guide to imitate. Rather they are here to help you see how different traders respond to, cope with, and overcome stressful events in their trading careers. Even if you don't relate to or identify with these traders' experiences, I am sure that you can learn from them. By reading through these profiles, perhaps you will be able to better understand how personality affects the way in which each individual handles stress, and you may gain some insights that will help you curb negative personality characteristics or enhance positive ones, in order to more productively handle the stress of the trading game.

## LIST MAKERS (ANALYTICAL THINKERS)

Generally, you can spot an analytical thinker from across the room. His desk, though crowded, most likely has some sense of order. Even if no one else can recognize it, there is likely to be a system that he is following in arranging his mass of paperwork, charts, and other materials. You may notice that he often has his head in a book or newspaper or spends a lot of time examining or creating charts or files.

When you talk with the analytical thinker about a problem, you notice that usually he likes to move from point to point in a very organized fashion. For instance, he will address the issue at hand, lay out all the options, discuss the pros and cons, and then draw what appears to be a logical conclusion. He may even have a chart or a list to demonstrate his thoughts. In fact, he is often creating lists—lists of things to do, things to think about, future ideas. It is not hard to see that the analytical thinker is likely to enjoy the data-gathering aspect of trading. He likes to learn about the companies and discover the important bits of news that other traders have nonchalantly dismissed. He enjoys researching the past history of a stock and making well-informed predictions of its future development. In fact, these are the analytical thinker's strengths.

Because of his deep desire to get all the information and to make the most informed decision possible, the analytical thinker has a tendency to procrastinate in terms of actually placing the trade. This is one of his weaknesses, and may point to perfectionism. He is constantly searching for more and better data and sometimes becomes so caught up in the process of digging deeper that he misses the open window of opportunity in which he should place the trade. In fact, many analytical traders are risk-averse. They are so attached to the process of gaining and organizing all the pertinent material that they can be late putting their knowledge to the test.

Let's take a look at a few examples.

### Analytical Thinker Who Wants to Fit In

Dalton's strength was his ability to analyze companies and combine his analysis with valuations as well as the short-term catalysts in the technology sector. However, this personality strength was severely weakened by another personality trait, his eagerness to be a part of the crowd, to belong. Because he wanted to fit in with the shorter-term model used by many of the traders in his firm, Dalton stopped doing the longer-term work that he liked and that he did so well. Because he tried to trade following the approach of others rather than staying with his strength, he weakened his chances for success and profitability.

After studying his past performances and seeing his mistake, he made the decision to move back toward a longer-term, deeply analytical approach to technology. He was making an effort to establish this model and considering whether adding additional analysts would eventually help him ramp up his capital usage.

## Analytical Thinker But Not a Manager

Chase was a problem solver. He liked to diagnose a problem and find a solution. He was also a lifelong learner. These strengths were very consistent with what he did well in his trading career—talking to companies, collecting information, and interacting with people he knew. However, they were not strengths that would help him in becoming a leader or a portfolio manager. By examining his strengths and weaknesses, Chase realized that he would most likely find more success as an analyst working under someone else rather than trying to be the manager himself.

## Analytical Thinking Gone Awry

Barrett was concerned about information overload and balancing his trading activities with his constant desire for more analytical work. Further inquiry suggested that Barrett was attempting to learn about too many companies at once and that he might be better off limiting himself. He would probably be better off building a model and learning all he could about one company. This would give him something to focus on, and he could do bits and pieces of his analysis throughout the day as well as in the evenings until he mastered the analytics. He could then apply the methodology he learned to the next company. He literally could build his understanding one stock at a time.

## Paralyzed Analytical Thinker

Dustin was a prime example of a risk-averse analytical trader. He believed in his technicals but was paralyzed while trading. In reviewing his statistics, it was clear that he had more winning days than losing days but that he lost twice as much on losing days as he made on winning days. He used very little capital, held his losers much too long, and did not press his winners even when he had conviction. (Forgive me if you think I mention this too often, but it is a pattern that sabotages not just analytical traders, but many other personality types as well.)

To combat this problem, I suggested that Dustin set up a plan to incrementally size his positions so that he could begin to use more of his capital and produce results without waiting for the "Eureka!" moment when it would all miraculously come together. By setting a modest $5,000 to $10,000 per day goal, he could try to find ways of making this target on a consistent basis. In addition, it might be beneficial for Dustin to specialize in a group of stocks, say 25, which he can get to know really well as opposed to trading everything but not really developing a fundamental edge in anything.

## Adventure Seeker (Impulsive Personality)

Most of us know at least one person who is a daredevil type. Mostly likely he has always been known as an adventure seeker or an impulsive personality. As a child he was the most likely kid in the neighborhood to be seen riding down the middle of the street on the handlebars of someone's bike. As a teenager he was probably taken to the emergency room more than once after accidents, and as an adult he may be known to bungee jump or skydive on weekends. Or he may show his impulsive streak in other ways. He may be the husband who spontaneously packs up the family and heads off to Vegas for the weekend or a devoted employee who abruptly quits after one especially frustrating day. In whatever form it manifests itself, impulsiveness seems to be an inborn quality for some, and it is perhaps one of the most dangerous personalities in the trading game.

Looking for constant thrills and self-gratification, impulsive traders are known to be good at thinking on their feet. They make quick decisions and love the excitement of the trading game. Unfortunately, their craving for constant action can lead them to venture into unwise trading moves and to develop a distaste for the more time-consuming and slower-paced tasks like information gathering. While they have no problem taking risk, they do have a problem managing it. Easily bored, adventure seekers grow distracted, especially when losing.

## Impulsive Actions and Anxiety

Felix was at a plateau in his trading career. He seemed to be getting nowhere fast. A closer examination of his recent trades suggested that he was playing defensively and impulsively. He took the pain in Company A and rode out the short that was being squeezed in his face. When the short started to work and his thesis was coming to fruition, he got scared and impulsively started to cover. He was sidetracked by the thought of losing and reduced the amount of profitability in his trades.

This became a pattern. He would become anxious as his trades were working. Instead of sticking to his original thesis (as it was playing out), he would panic. Afraid of losing his profit for the year, he would start covering instead of riding out the short and taking his full measure of reward.

I likened this behavior to the so-called sucker answer on a multiple-choice test. Of five answers, two appear to be right. The sucker answer is the easier answer, which leads the anxious test taker to impulsively pick it. The more skilled test taker goes for the answer that is counterintuitive, rides out the discomfort, picks the tougher of the two, and ends up acing the test.

Felix accepted this observation—that he was acting on impulses and going for the "sucker trade." Having begun to understand how and why he was acting this way, he determined to begin to take more time to think through his decisions before getting out of his trades. I will return to Felix in Chapter 12, where I discuss shorting in greater detail.

## Impulsive Reactions and a Failure to Manage

Pablo demonstrated how self-destructive impulsiveness could be. When his analysts failed to give him the ideas that he needed to meet his goal, he said, "If you can't give me ideas, I will find them myself." Instead of figuring out what his analysts needed to do and how he could motivate them, he stopped managing altogether. His do-it-yourself approach proved disastrous. Instead of managing the process in a rational way, he went ahead with his trades without the sufficient work necessary and paid with big losses. Upon further consideration, Pablo realized that he did a bad job not just of managing the portfolio but also of managing the risk. "I failed to manage all these people," he acknowledged.

Unfortunately, however, instead of taking the time to establish precautions so that this kind of mistake wouldn't happen again, Pablo refused to acknowledge the root of the problem—his impulsive nature.

"No doubt the postmortem has to be done," he said. "It's not something I want to distract myself with at this point. I would much prefer to say, 'I have messed up. Something went wrong. I will figure that out in a minute.'"

In the end, Pablo blamed the analysts themselves for the losses, and still neglected to do what was necessary to create a winning team.

## INTUITIVE THINKERS

Some people—skeptics might categorize them as touchy-feely types—just seem to be governed more by their emotions than their intellect. They "feel" everything, and this isn't necessarily bad. Known as intuitive thinkers, these are the people you meet who might say things like, "This is going to be a great day. I can just feel it." And normally they are right. They place great value on their instincts. Often intuitive thinkers seem to have developed a sixth sense that they employ on a regular basis.

Intuitive traders might seem to have the golden touch. Whereas they may not be consistently profitable, they have a knack for huge wins every now and again. Yet, if you asked them how they make a judgment, they might not be able to give you much of an answer. "I just had a gut instinct," they would respond.

While some people want to dismiss their instincts as a "bunch of emotional baloney," there seems to be some validity to them. For example, everyone has long understood that some mothers seem to instinctively be able to know things about their children—when they are in danger, when they are upset, when something is medically wrong. Few people question that type of intuition, but many have serious doubts about the value of intuition in careers such as trading.

Of course, there are people who use intuition to direct almost every area of their lives, but if you look more closely you will find that the most successful intuitive thinkers are those who act intuitively on the basis of experience. Let's go back to mothers. How does a mother intuitively know so many things about her child? The answer is because she knows her child so well, most likely better than anyone else. Sometimes there are things about the child that she has processed and stored in her brain that she is not even aware of having learned (for example, the noises the child makes while sleeping). Later, when something changes (she walks past the child's room and hears a strange gurgling/snorting sound), a little light goes off in her head. Something is not right. Why is her child making that noise in his sleep? Is he sick? Her intuition is based on her experience.

The same can be said with the most intuitive traders. Most of them have developed an intuition based on years of experience. They have, even sometimes unconsciously, stored vast amounts of information about how the markets will react under certain circumstances, or how certain stocks will respond to certain events. When an event happens, they are able to respond so quickly that it appears they are doing it without any thought at all, but actually their brains are processing previously stored data.

## Using Intuition Wisely

Aiden considered himself a very relaxed trader and was confused by his recent poor performance. He tried to understand the relevance of his gut reactions and how to wisely use his intuitive thoughts in his trading game. Sometimes, he said, he had "an overall gut feeling, which makes me want to get into a trade without having necessarily done the work." He admitted that he had become "more stubborn" in these cases than he had been traditionally.

"If I have a view, I will tend to stick to that view," he said. "I am willing to let losses run in the areas where I have the highest conviction. Sometimes it turns around, and I will make an awful lot of money because I do have an insight. Sometimes I am completely wrong, and it ends up costing a lot of money."

After talking with Aiden, I found that in most of his losing trades he was making two mistakes. First, he believed in something for which he had no basis and no validation, and second, he risked more than he should on those beliefs.

I pointed out to Aiden that part of using his intuitive feelings requires a certain amount of work. I suggested that he start by determining (with the help of his risk manager) an appropriate amount of risk that he could take in these trades. Then he should keep track of how several of these gut reactions actually turned out in the end. If he discovered that many of his reactions proved fruitful, he could be assured that there was probably some basis for his feelings and could feel more confident in following these intuitions. "But you have to do the work to justify the gut feeling," I told him.

Aiden understood. "I have to make enough time to do the work quickly enough to find out whether or not the gut instinct is right, then get into the position before everyone else does," he said.

An important part of using gut instincts is learning to pay more attention to the results. If the results tell a trader that something isn't working, then he may need to reconsider whether his intuition is proving beneficial. The worst thing an intuitive trader can do is to think, "My intuition is always right. Something is just wrong with the market."

Basically, it doesn't matter what a trader feels or what he wants. It matters what he has to do to survive. Sometimes that means acting contrary to the way he feels. For intuitive traders, this may require asking for help from another trader who can be a mentor, a coach, or an assistant.

At the end of the day, a trader has to know his strengths and weaknesses. For Aiden and other intuitive traders, the most important reminder is that gut instincts are not an excuse to bypass the work but an impetus for digging deeper. The point of the trading game is to make money—not justify feelings. There is nothing wrong with being an intuitive trader. Intuitive traders just need to apply those feelings toward the service of their goals.

## OPTIMIST/PESSIMIST/REALIST

Traders who are overly optimistic can find themselves battling a problem of overtrading and trading ineffectively when the information is not there to support the action. However, traders who are pessimistic by nature may be risk-averse or find that they are unable to pick themselves up after great losses.

Perhaps what's required is a healthy dose of both pessimism and optimism. Realists understand that losses are inevitable. However, they know that successes could accrue if they develop a realistic plan of action and learn from their mistakes. Part of being a realist is utilizing effective risk management tools. Another is creating realistic objectives and taking the necessary steps to reach those objectives.

In general, it is better to be an optimist. Whereas optimists have to guard against rash behavior, pessimists in general give up too easily—a trait that will get you nowhere fast in the trading game.

## Pessimist and Retrospective Distress

Stephan, an impatient type, was inclined to get out of positions too fast because he was certain that they wouldn't go the way his analysis suggested they would. This led to a lot of retrospective distress when he reviewed how much he could have made.

Because of his pessimistic outlook, he hadn't developed a game plan in terms of his profit objectives. He designed no trading strategy in terms of what kind of results he expected to get from his trades, how to size the positions, and how many positions to put on relative to the work he had done.

His negative personality characteristics were holding him back. Without a trading strategy to follow, he was trading willy-nilly based on how he felt and missing out on a lot of profit as a result. To combat the problem, I suggested Stephan get together with another trader who had a definite trading and portfolio management strategy. By taking the time to learn how to create his own strategy, he would have a plan of action to follow regardless of his feelings.

## Pessimism, Passivity, and Panic

Some traders still have difficulty even when they have a strategy to follow. Tony was a pessimist who had a problem with passivity. Because he constantly waited for guidance, he failed to do the work that would keep him on track. His negative thinking deterred him from digging deeply or from getting bigger in his better trades. In addition, it contributed to his unwillingness to stay longer in winning trades.

In discussing the issues, I encouraged him to be more proactive and aggressive and to keep doing the work, putting his best ideas forward and increasing his profitability so as to earn the opportunity to run more capital. He heeded my suggestions. By keeping a journal of his thoughts and trading decisions, he realized he was inclined to panic when stocks went against him. He began learning how to handle his stress in a more productive manner.

## Dangers of an Optimist

Jayson could, at times, be considered a giddy optimist. In his euphoric attitude of "things will get even better," Jayson seemed to forget to use common sense and ended up giving back a lot of profits. His main problem was not taking his profits at the right time. Instead he held on, even when everything indicated it was time to get out, and he wound up losing instead of gaining. In fact, Jayson actually had a history of doing better when he started in the hole. It was then that his optimistic personality helped him work up the nerve to think the best while hunkering down and trading cautiously.

Fortunately, Jayson detected this tendency and made adjustments. He started to manage his risk better by reducing his expectations and getting out of trades on time. He tried building up a cushion before making bigger bets. His discipline and cautiousness helped him remain cognizant of how he could become overly optimistic and desire unrealistically large profits when he was trading in the zone.

## ARE YOU CONFIDENT OR INSECURE?

As we discussed in the previous chapter, there is a fine line between confidence and arrogance, and also between humility and insecurity. Whether your self-esteem is a result of predisposition or life experiences, your level of confidence can affect your trading game.

A trader must have an appropriate level of confidence to ensure that he has the stamina to stay in the business. But sometimes overconfidence can be an indication of fear. People with poor self-esteem or those who are very fearful often mask their fears by putting on a charade—an act of competence and control. Unfortunately, when the real pressure comes, that kind of confidence is of little benefit, and the true colors show.

Trading is so stressful that even traders who generally show great poise can still find their confidence shaken. One of the best ways to gain confidence in trading is to develop and carry through on a well-devised plan of action. At regular intervals, you can sketch out a course based on current patterns, and at the end of a period of time—or when there is a clear indication of change—you can correct, enhance, or even scrap this advance-planning guide.

## Insecurity and Loss

Joel was frustrated with his trading. He was getting out of positions when they went against him only to be disappointed when they moved up and it was too late to get back in. At the same time, he tended to get out of his winners too fast so that he had fewer winning days. Adding to the problem was that Joel was older than many of the other beginning traders, and he and others seemed to expect that he would be further ahead than he was. Joel needed a good boost of confidence to help get him going again.

Because of his insecurity, Joel spent too much time on the analysis of his companies rather than trying to be the trader he once was. For Joel to overcome his insecurity, he needed to build his psychological confidence. In one scenario, he could build up a cushion of P&L and remind himself that expectations should not be a consideration in designing his game plan.

## Insecurity and Overintellectualization

Henry also was battling insecurity. A very cautious trader, he was down 3 percent and was using only about 20 percent of his capital. Further conversations with him suggested he was being very literal-minded and analytical about things in general. His lack of confidence led him to overthink and second-guess everything. He had a hard time seeing the forest for the trees. Unfortunately, while he understood his thinking habits, he believed that his overintellectualization was a benefit and that it had kept him from making mistakes in the past. By trying to avoid looking at his daily P&L on the screen and to move toward his longer-term, value-oriented model with less preoccupation and concern about short-term trading, he started to restore his confidence and to trade a little more smoothly.

## MAKE THE MOST OF YOUR PERSONALITY

Your personality is an intricate and unique pattern of possibilities, and it is up to you to determine how to make your traits work best in your trading. The goal is not to change your personality. You are who you are. If you are stubborn by nature, don't seek to change that characteristic. Learn to use it to your advantage. You might, for example, rely on your stubbornness to keep you in trades until they reach complete fruition, especially if you are a deep value investor and have done a lot of fundamental work. If you are by nature an unorganized person, does that mean that you can't be a disciplined trader with an organized plan of action? No, because you don't have to be disciplined all the time. By having a detailed trading strategy, you are more likely to stay disciplined within your trades even if discipline is not your strong suit.

A frightened person may not be able to shed his fears, especially overnight. However, he can make adjustments so that his fears don't hold him back. Gerry, for example, demonstrated the desire to use more capital in the coming year, but he realized that he was somewhat more cautious than he needed to be. After considering his personality, he understood that he was risk-averse, and he sought some methodology for breaking through this so that he could perform better. He had the desire to take more risk and to hold on to winners longer when he had a fundamental edge, but he didn't know how to overcome his caution.

My advice was that instead of trying to change his conservative personality, he should learn to be more flexible. For example, instead of trying to make himself stay in a trade that he feared was going to become a loser, he could exit the trade but give himself permission to get back into the same trade if he found out that he was wrong and saw that the trade would continue to work.

More important, I suggested that it would be easier to concentrate his efforts on getting bigger in his high-conviction ideas when he first got into the position and was confident about the possible price action. By increasing his size in trades in which he was already confident, he could reap bigger wins without taxing his cautious nature.

Some traders may also benefit from having other people—particularly someone who is opposite in personality—help in areas of weakness. A trader so paralyzed by fear that he cannot bring himself to place a trade can do the work, and then ask a more confident trader to actually place the call for him. Or a trader who has trouble with organizational skills may want to hire an assistant or associate to handle the more detailed tasks that he cannot seem to finish.

Unfortunately, many traders are taught to dismiss their subjective reactions or ignore their basic personality traits. I think it makes more sense to encourage you to use these personal characteristics to develop better decision-making skills. Your personal experiences and personality features can offer valuable information that you cannot derive by any other means.

## A WINNING PERSONALITY

If personality is so deeply involved in how a trader handles stress and in the trading decisions he makes, the question then becomes, "Do winning traders have a certain *type* of personality?" The answer is no. No one type of personality is necessarily better for trading than all the others. However, winning traders do have several things in common, and one is the ability to objectively review how their personality is affecting their trading game.

A winning trader often has a combination of personality traits—some of which come naturally, some of which are learned. For example, a winning trader will understand the importance of digging deeply for information before placing a trade, whether or not he is a born analyst. In addition, a winning trader, while not acting impulsively, will be ready to respond quickly when needed and not be afraid to take appropriate risks.

You can become a winning trader by learning to be attuned to your bodily reactions, so that you'll recognize the signs that point to taking a certain action. By tuning in to your own psyche, you won't react on the basis of your emotions but will use those emotions to help determine your next moves.

In addition, most traders have at some point experienced what it is like to be in the zone, when everything seems to be coming together exactly as it should. Most traders have also found themselves in the middle of a trade that they just sense is not going to work. For some reason that they can't put their finger on, something just doesn't feel right. When winning traders find themselves in this place, they know how to read their own emotions and feelings and incorporate those into their trading decisions. While these emotions should not be an alternative to the more analytical means of decision making, they can complement the process.

Because the market is constantly changing and the future is never 100 percent predictable, no number of models or rules will allow a trader to be correct the majority of the time. It is imperative that traders use every single advantage that they have, including their vast amount of personal experience, which is stored and retrieved most often through their instincts and emotions.

While you will not naturally have all the strengths of every great trader, you can most assuredly learn from them and learn to imitate not their style or personality but their winning actions. Successful traders succeed regardless of the market conditions and do so because they have learned to enhance their natural abilities, strengthen or diminish the importance of their natural weaknesses, and develop skills that they currently lack.

One of the gravest errors you can make is to ignore or justify your personality characteristics—especially those that can be seen in a negative light. You won't fool anyone, most especially yourself. Instead, utilize your most promising tools to develop a unique edge. Rather than allow your personality traits to control you, allow yourself to recognize the signals your personality sends out, and then use those characteristics to guide you into more productive trading patterns.

Here are five things you can do:

1. If you are too analytic, increase your size incrementally on trades.
2. If you are intuitive, make sure you justify your hunches with facts.
3. If you are insecure, build up your P&L until your confidence returns.
4. If you are a pessimist, keep a journal so you recall your successes.
5. If you are too optimistic, discipline yourself to be aware of going over-board.

# CHAPTER 7

# Ego and Obstinacy

*S*anford was what I call an idea person. He liked to "connect the dots," look at things from a different angle, find the simplicity behind the complex, or find the complexity behind the simple. Perhaps that was why he enjoyed and was so good at the game of golf—where the simple concept of hitting a small ball into a small hole becomes riddled with complexities such as the type of driver being used, the course being played, the angle the ball needs to be hit from, how the weather conditions affect all this, and so on.

As a world traveler constantly in search of new sights and adventures, Sanford's drive for ideas was fed only by a discontentment with stability. He was always seeking achievement—new, greater, unique achievements—perhaps in an effort to maintain the image he had carefully and painstakingly built.

But interestingly, the pursuit of new goals didn't mean that Sanford lived for the future. In fact, he was prone to living in the past—drawing his ideas, goals, and plans from history; placing great importance on his own experiences; and relying heavily on previous lessons to plan for future events. Combining this information with his what-if types of questions led him to strategize his actions and then doggedly and obstinately pursue a clear destination—before he quickly set another.

Given Sanford's interesting mix of personal characteristics, it would seem that he is an ideal trader. He knows how to set a goal, define a strategy, and pursue his vision with zest. But all of this searching for answers and planning for results has, in Sanford's case, led to an overconfident ego that sometimes gets in the way of successful trading. While his desire to find new ideas leads him to flesh out the fundamental principles behind a stock's story, his dependency on his own past experiences makes it hard for him to see the relevance of the suggestions of others (such as his risk manager). His need to understand the culture motivates him to keep looking for explanations about why things are the way they are so as to maintain his sense of confidence. His independent, self-confident nature, while an asset at times, makes it hard for him to adapt to the expectations of others, even when he is in a drawdown.

## A STUBBORN NATURE

One of Sanford's strengths is his desire to search out and discover the story behind a stock. He is willing to go the extra mile to discern what everyone else may have missed, to put the pieces together, to make the picture fuller, sharper, and more distinct. In addition, his need for new ideas and new information makes it difficult for him to trade anything unless he has a high conviction about it. While not bad in and of themselves, Sanford's statistics reveal how these tendencies are causing him to miss winning trades and stay in losing trades too long.

At first glance it is obvious that he is performing very poorly. His total P&L for the year is negative $6 million. His return on allocated and invested capital is down 4 percent. While he has 53 percent of up days, his win/loss (W/L) ratio is .83, suggesting that he loses more in his losing trades than he makes in his winning trades.

Looking more closely at his performance by holding period, analysis reveals that he has been profitable in stocks that he has held from 6 days to 60 days but that he has lost a substantial amount of money in both longs and shorts in positions he has held for longer than 60 days—down about $7 million. Of that, $6.5 million is losses in longs and $493,000 in shorts.

Interestingly, most of his losses are in the sector he specializes in, suggesting that he has held on to these positions because of *belief* in the positions even when they weren't working in his favor. Listen to his own description of his mind-set during such a trade:

"I feel it in my gut. I feel it in my brain. I can't wait to wake up the next day. Everything changes. The line of my body changes. I stand up straighter. I am an athlete when it comes to this stuff," he explained.

Why would Sanford so diligently seek after losing stocks? Why would he believe so strongly in something that is clearly costing him money? Because he has invested so much time in the information-gathering process, searching and finding information to support his thesis.

Unfortunately, when that thesis turns out to be wrong, he has a hard time admitting it to himself or others and stays in the trade anyway—hoping beyond hope that it will turn around. While holding on to losing positions for a longer time frame may work in a mutual fund setting where relative performance against an index and longer holding periods hold sway, this is not a successful plan of action in the more dynamic shorter-term, profit-oriented hedge fund where Sanford is employed.

Obviously, Sanford needs to approach his positions more diligently. He needs to be willing to get into some positions in which he has somewhat lower conviction and to get out of higher-conviction positions that aren't working. This won't happen without considerable effort, because he is working against an embedded personality trait.

## Case Study in Obstinacy

In this conversation, Sanford and I are discussing stocks in his sector. Listen to Sanford's confidence in how much information he has about these stocks versus the average trader. As you read, consider his sense of confidence in the information he has gathered versus his ability to be flexible should that information prove faulty or should circumstances change. Ask yourself if Sanford sounds willing to get out should this trade go bad. I pick up this conversation with that particular thought in mind.

| | |
|---|---|
| **Kiev:** | Everybody is trapped, limited, or constrained by his own thought processes. |
| **Sanford:** | Nevertheless—and this isn't a comment coming out of my ego or anything else—when I hear anybody picking up a line out of an article or publication about how these stocks behave in general or trying to understand whether somebody actually knows what they are talking about in a particular sector, I am so past that conversation it's almost startling. I am just so far into the subject it's actually hard to get all the way back and put it into context. |
| **K:** | You are saying that you really understand these companies. |
| **S:** | There are literally a handful of people in the industry who have been successful at investing in this category. Between this time frame and the July earnings, I am going to have rotated everything and do the opposite for the second half. |
| **K:** | Why is it going to go down in the second half? |
| **S:** | The business is going to stay high. They're going to stay like this. They are going to stay picking up all the way through the fourth quarter. |
| **K:** | So why would you get out here? |

S:      Because the stocks are going to reflect this at a big banking conference that is coming up in a month or so. People are going to start to sell them.

K:      You don't think the momentum will continue long?

S:      It could get overbought, and that's why it would take a month to rotate it out.

K:      So, you don't want to ignore the market.

S:      Exactly, if the market keeps taking it.

K:      What about putting trading stops in?

S:      It's a great idea.

K:      The way the market looks, people could get overexcited. You don't want to get trapped by your thesis—that you "know" it's going down. While you have a strategy geared to what's going on, you need to protect your profits and increase the chance of making more money, because, given our human nature, you might be inclined to get out too soon.

S:      You're right about that. The reason that I was able to make the money that I made in these stocks in the 1990s was that I was so close to companies that it just kept getting better internally. The reason I was able to keep the stocks is that they would double again. Everybody thought I was crazy, and I said, "You don't understand."

K:      You just hung in.

S:      It just kept getting better.

K:      That was then, and this is now. You don't want to hang on to that belief.

S:      No, my belief is that I will trade out of the stock. I actually think the industry is much more mature and has far more cyclicality, and this year will be down, and I am getting out. I will get out in June and July. Hopefully, I will be able to catch some of that.

Did you catch the broad hints of Sanford's stubborn streak? Did you notice how he referred to his past experience to justify his current decisions? Did the conversation lead you to believe that if the circumstances warranted Sanford could or would get out in time?

Sanford has to learn to admit when he is wrong, which is in direct conflict with his ego issues. He has to bite the bullet and change course when his trades turn and his thesis proves wrong. He also needs to know when enough is enough and not needlessly postpone the creation of a trade in an effort to obtain all the information there is to know. By reviewing his statistics and being aware of these weaknesses, he will, one hopes, take measures to help correct them.

## REFUSAL TO ACCEPT COMMANDS

Unfortunately, Sanford's self-confidence is also one of his biggest personal obstacles. One facet manifests itself in his appearance—expensive suits and ties, the dress-for-success look. Within the context of his trading career, Sanford is constantly battling his intellect, his pride, and his need for overly large wins, which manifests in his need to look busy and smart.

While confidence in one's abilities is often an asset, overconfidence in a trader is not going to work to his favor. Overconfident traders tend to put too much emphasis on their own abilities and have too little concern for the opinions or suggestions of others. This is evident in Sanford's inability to accept risk management requests. In fact, Sanford is so self-consumed at times that he fails to even comprehend the need for outside influences.

For example, after one particular incident when risk management asked Sanford to cut his risk, he seemed relatively calm but somewhat perplexed. He claimed that if he hadn't brought down his capital he would have made more money than he did in the past week when he was up over $1 million.

"I don't understand why risk management is always asking me to cut down just as I am about to be rewarded," he complained. "I have followed the limits laid out in my contract, and I am down only 5 percent on the $200,000 buying power. I think there ought to be more debate about what I am doing with my portfolio rather than just being told to cut things down."

I tried to explain how capital preservation was important to the picture others had of him and offered the idea that his capital would increase as his performance improved, but he continued to argue that his statistics had improved considerably since March or April, when he was down $11 million. He compared himself to other traders and blamed his losses on "aberrations attributable to a couple of bad stock picks."

Basically, Sanford follows a set of rules to determine whether to get bigger or smaller depending on how the stock is moving. These rules allow him to trade in and out of positions based on the percentage moves that the stocks make. While this kind of system looks good on the surface, it actually leads to automatic decisions based strictly on percentage moves that he has set up to satisfy the needs of risk management. For Sanford, this is just another way to avoid taking responsibility for his trades and to have an excuse to give risk management if things go wrong. His system doesn't take into account the reality of the markets and how circumstances are prone to change. Sanford refuses to acknowledge that traders must retain a measure of flexibility or heed the advice of good counsel.

## DIFFICULTY WITH MANAGEMENT

As you can imagine, because of Sanford's analytical nature, inflated ego, and natural stubborn streak, he is not one to back down from an argument or take the advice (or commands) of others very easily. Add to that his constant desire to look better and smarter than everyone else, and you have a dangerous cocktail when it comes to how he interacts with management.

### Case Study on Controlling Obstinacy

Here, I am trying to prepare Sanford for a conversation he is to have with his risk manager. Despite the fact that Sanford reluctantly followed the risk manager's previous advice and benefited from it, he continues to argue that he could manage better. He refuses to acknowledge the risk manager's positions and debates the manager's every request. In addition, he fails to acknowledge how his attempts at "helping" the risk manager are not only unwarranted but unwanted. He has an ego that's getting in the way of making wise choices.

**Sanford:** I have twice as many shorts as longs. My longs have done a little better. Of course, I have a load of winning percentages on a career basis. Nobody's shorts are working. I mean, let's cut the numbers. Let's actually do some work. What does that number mean? If you have twice as many shorts, it doesn't really mean anything. What they should be looking at is my percentage of winners on the long book. It doesn't look so bad. My shorts don't work. My percentage of winners looks bad. It takes too much time to cut the numbers properly. I know that the firm manager's view of this is a highly experienced, highly thoughtful view. I know that the risk manager sees a ton of these. So they can make comparisons because they see so much there. Unless they're willing to add specificity to whatever they're doing, they can still ad-lib.

**Kiev:** You mean you have to add understanding of the specific company information or the feel for the company?

**S:** I am talking about what *they* respond to.

**K:** What do you mean by "add specificity"?

**S:** Actually go into the portfolio. Their view is that any percentage is lower than it should be. It's probably because I have twice as many shorts as I do longs, and there aren't many portfolios like that in this shop. It's the worst of the firm. Let's add some detail to that.

| | |
|---|---|
| **K:** | What do you mean by that? |
| **S:** | What does it mean if you have this many extra positions? What would it look like? It would be very different. |
| **K:** | Are you saying the firm manager is not clarifying it in terms of making suggestions? |
| **S:** | There is no discussion. That's what I am saying. Maybe it's because they have too little time. |
| **K:** | So, you are upset because they have not told you how you could have traded differently? |
| **S:** | We're not getting into what the data actually reflects. |
| **K:** | But when you look at your stats, you agree with the conclusion that you should have gotten out of some of those losses sooner. Correct? |
| **S:** | Yes, and I am managing the portfolio here very differently now. It's much tighter, much more oriented to how the market is behaving, much more oriented to the macro. I had to take capital down. I want this to work so badly. I think I can add a lot to this place. I think I am going to make a lot of money. I think I can help them think more thoughtfully about management and how to manage. Maybe that's a conversation they don't want to have. |
| **K:** | That's probably not what drives them. The conversation you need to have with the firm manager will be a little bit more trading-oriented. The risk manager is going to want to hear that you're on board with his way of seeing the world. So my view is that you should cooperate and get the license to go trade. Then you continue your communication with the firm manager and pass along your ideas to him when the time comes. |
| **S:** | Tell me what I should expect. |
| **K:** | Most of the time traders cooperate. My gut would tell me that the risk manager is not interested in learning how he can better manage. He is probably more interested in getting you to say that he's right. Ever since your previous conversation, you have been trying to do what he said and you have gotten it down flat. So, you should appreciate his help. That would be my recommendation. He is not looking for a devil's advocate. |
| **S:** | I am sure the systems here are very good, but what's required is an added layer of discussion that does not exist. |
| **K:** | I am not sure that this is the conversation to elucidate how things ought to improve. I may be wrong. He may ask you, "What do we need to do?" Then he may say, "You've got it! I will put that in place. That's great!" But I don't think so. He tends to be a little more bureaucratic, a command-and-control type. So |

my sense would be that you should do it the way he wants to do it. The firm manager might be the guy to have that conversation with. That's my sense. I would recommend cooperating. Do you hear what I am saying?

S:      Yes, and I appreciate your help with this.

K:      I don't think this is the kind of thing you want to hear. I think you feel that you are right and they are wrong or that they are inadequate. I am trying to tell you that I don't think there is going to be an audience for that type of conversation.

S:      Right. I can adjust it.

K:      I would be more political, unless you don't care.

S:      I do care. I care deeply. I had an extraordinary experience this year. I can adjust. What I really want to do is have a conversation with the risk manager where we can move forward.

K:      Be cooperative so that you can get the space to go back and do what you have to do. If you go in fighting, he is going to react, and you're going to react. Am I getting through?

S:      Yes.

K:      You would probably rather fight than not. I am saying, "Don't fight!"

S:      I've got it!

K:      You have to acknowledge his wisdom.

S:      I want to give him something that is sort of useful. He can decide whether to regard or disregard it.

K:      He is *not* looking for input like that. He doesn't want your help in doing his job. He just wants to know that you're going to listen to the program that he has prescribed. I know it's tough. Your inclination is to swing for the fences. It seems to me that you are going to once again go in saying, "This is my view. I just want to tell you how you ought to run the business."

S:      That's not what I was going to do.

K:      Didn't you say that you want to give him advice that is going to help him?

S:      This conversation is about my experience this year. This conversation is going to be a very constructive conversation. It is going to be about my relationship with the firm and his relationship with me, and how all that is going to go forward. He had a significant impact on how I turned the corner. I just want to tell him where there are one or two things—small adjustments that could be made to a process that is already in place.

K:      There is the potential that those "adjustments" will be perceived by the risk manager as criticism.

S:      Okay, maybe it's not the right setting.

K:      He is coming to talk about *your* experience.

S:      We are going to sort out the end of the year and next year. That's going to take a while to go through. My guess is there will be an opportunity to reflect.

K:      Maybe you are not getting it.

S:      I genuinely believe this is where people respect each other. I am not a lapdog. I have some very valid things to say, come what may.

K:      Okay. Good luck!

In this next conversation Sanford expresses some of his frustration about the management of the firm and his need for a certain amount of feedback or information that he feels he is not receiving. He believes that if he had been given certain information by the firm when he first started, it would have helped him to adjust more quickly in a new trading environment.

Kiev:      How have things gone for you since you came here?

Sanford:      I didn't have a lot of portfolio management experience when I came, and I think it would have been more helpful to have more structure built into the firm. You have a lot of autonomy here, but it would almost be nice if you had some type of structure where for the first three months or six months new people were given a little bit more guidance—more mentoring, more information about processes. Here it's a little bit disorganized. At other places if you walk in they say, "Here is a broker list, salespeople, sales traders, and other contacts we have." It seems like you have to find all that stuff out for yourself here. It would be nice if there were a little bit more structure or just procedures that were in place.

K:      How about in terms of the autonomy? Do you like that?

S:      I do. It's good in that you definitely have to be a self-starter and someone who is pretty disciplined. You are responsible for your P&L. If you have a bad month, no one else is going to help make it up for you.

K:      Does having responsibility for your P&L add a motivational factor to it?

S:      The harder you work, the more money you should make. The more dedicated you are, the more you put your procedures in place.

As Sanford's comments indicate, he is at least now learning how to approach management in a more productive way. He is also learning to prioritize his need to know and to curb unnecessary questions.

Upon understanding Sanford's personality, management is also learning how to better help him by explaining the culture of the firm in which he works and encouraging him to ask questions at the appropriate times (such as weekly meetings and one-on-one consultations).

Sanford went on to tell me that he had improved in his ability to relate to management and to accept the suggestions of others. He had been the type who offered numerous suggestions to others and at first wondered why the head of his new firm did not respond. He said he now realizes that the chief gets bombarded with ideas from all directions. Now that he has grasped the notion of autonomy that prevails at the firm, he feels he needs to be more aggressive in simply putting his own ideas into play.

Slowly but surely Sanford is learning to direct his aggressive tendencies in a more productive way. In effect, he is beginning to understand how his personality affects his trading and has been consciously changing his trading style. Not only is he interacting with management in a more beneficial way, he is also taking losses more quickly, continuing to size up good ideas, and learning to take what the market gives him.

"Everything is a reflection of yourself," he said. "If you look at the market and the market seems to be doing X, it's not because the market is actually doing that but because that's the way you always view the market. Your first reaction can sometimes be the wrong one."

In the past Sanford was guided strictly by fundamental analysis. Now he has started letting the market guide him toward more flexibility. Through the use of journaling, he has begun to see mistakes more clearly and to learn from negative as well as positive past experiences. He forced himself to learn to admit when he was wrong, and that was a big step.

When management recognizes someone's strengths, when those at the top understand that some people don't respond well to command-and-control approaches, the smart ones try enroll the recalcitrant strays in the process intellectually so that they buy into the idea of conforming to risk management perspectives. Smart management also takes into consideration suggestions such as Sanford proposed to set up strict guidelines for new hires for the first few months until they adjust to the absolute performance standards of a long/short hedge fund. After a period of adhering to such guidelines, the successful trader might be better able to take 10 to 15 percent positions with greater impunity.

Despite improvements, Sanford is far from mastering the game of trading. In fact, he was down for his first year and struggled. Still, he didn't give up. The more he learned about his own personality, the more he could see how certain characteristics improve or weaken his game. Of course, all this—both the ups and downs—adds to the excitement of the trading game, and these ego-driven people such as Sanford respond in typical fashion. As Sanford commented, "It keeps you excited and driving to find that extra data point or come up with that new idea."

# CHAPTER 8

# Fear and Failure

*T*heodore was the kind of fellow who could make everyone in a room feel at ease instantly. Yet behind Theodore's congenial personality was a haunted trader whose past mistakes kept him from living up to his current potential.

At a more successful time in Theodore's career, he had faced a battle with anger that had cost him a lot—not in terms of money but in the form of personal relationships. Although Theodore eventually created a new life for himself personally, his past still bound him. Now, despite his desire for achievement and recognition, this self-motivated and hardworking trader faced the difficult task of overcoming an inherent fear of success. He was concerned that if he succeeded he might he might revert to his earlier angry, driven personality. He was looking for a way to remain congenial yet to reach the level of success that would satisfy him.

By his own account, Theodore was once a "golden boy" of trading. "I was 21 and running a huge commodity book, which was the fourth biggest such book in the world," he explained. "I actually went backwards because I wanted to leave. It didn't look like it was the right place to be. So I left and took a step down with regard to my career position. Six months later, I was the boss of the person who hired me. I was just very good, and I knew I was very good."

After another job change, Theodore was in the running for a partnership. But then some decisions were made that affected him negatively. "I was mad, so I just went and got a job somewhere else." After a series of career choices, Theodore eventually wound up managing others more than trading. Looking back, he associates that successful time in his life with the angry feelings he developed during it.

"If I am honest, I didn't have the most successful personal life between the ages of 20 and 30, but I had a very successful career. Then from 30 to 40 I had a very good personal life, but my career didn't really go anywhere," he said. Naturally, Theodore would like to have more success as a trader without giving up his happy family life. Now in his forties, he would like to start pushing the envelope careerwise, but he did not want to compromise his marriage. We talked about ways in which he could learn to handle things in a more compartmentalized way, so he did not take on time-consuming work functions that might spill over into his personal life.

## AFRAID TO WIN

Afraid that he would fall back into bad habits, Theodore is failing to truly commit himself to his trading game. He believes that if he pursues his goals wholeheartedly, he will be putting his personal relationships at risk. What he hasn't discovered is that if he wants to, he can have both—a successful personal life and a successful professional life.

Although Theodore has a deliberative nature and is constantly assessing the risks of every situation, this is one area in which he is failing to size things up in a realistic way. The lessons he learned from his past mistakes—both personally and professionally—can actually help him succeed in a greater way than before. His desire to succeed does not have to take a backseat to his fears of becoming angry or succeeding at the cost of his family relationships.

### Case Study on Fear Factors

In the following conversation you will begin to understand Theodore's reluctance to get bigger in his trading. While we don't specifically discuss his fear of success at this point, I want you to begin to hear in Theodore's own words how he sidesteps the fact that he is not trading at a level that will help him succeed. Watch carefully for phrases about getting out of positions too soon, not being as big as he needs to be, and having only 5 percent positions in his high-conviction ideas, all of which indicate he is not trading up to his potential or are excuses for not sizing his positions bigger. Listen as I begin to draw Theodore's attention to the need for more risk and bigger wins.

**Kiev:** How much money are you running?
**Theodore:** About $250 million.
**K:** What's your target?

| | |
|---|---|
| **T:** | My target is $25 million with a 10 percent return per year. That's an achievable number. These are tough targets, and I can make $15 million, but I would be happy to make $10 million. |
| **K:** | So when you say $25 million, do you divide that by months? Are you trying to make more than $2 million a month? |
| **T:** | I would like to make $2 million a month. |
| **K:** | Do you do that by weeks or days? |
| **T:** | My basic time frame is the month. That's what we get judged on. The report goes out in a month. |
| **K:** | What sector are you trading? |
| **T:** | I trade anything that is commodity related—mining, steel, airlines, cars, and stuff like that. I also trade oil, steel, and gold. |
| **K:** | Does $250 million give you $500 million buying power? |
| **T:** | Yes. I can leverage it to $500 million, but in this market I don't particularly want to. |
| **K:** | Do you run it hedged? |
| **T:** | Pretty much. I am 30 percent net short at the moment. |
| **K:** | Is the market up or down? |
| **T:** | Down, but again there are a lot of instances where I have been doing nothing and spinning my wheels. |
| **K:** | Do you size your position commensurate with your objectives? Are you as big as you need to be to make that $2 million? |
| **T:** | I am now. I was getting out of it before. |
| **K:** | Are you also sized in terms of your level of conviction? |
| **T:** | Yes. |
| **K:** | High conviction, with what percent? |
| **T:** | High conviction is 5 percent. |
| **K:** | Could it be bigger? |
| **T:** | It could. But in beta-adjusted terms, because I do volatile stocks, it's actually probably more like 8 percent. I have net for 15 percent short of steel stocks, which beta adjusted is more like 20 percent. That is less empowering, because the stocks move 2 to 3 percent a day. |
| **K:** | Are you up for the year? |
| **T:** | Now, sort of, broadly in line with where I have been. |
| **K:** | How long have you been trading? |
| **T:** | I came in February. When I came here everybody had had a 5 percent January. So I missed the easy money. They all basically lost that 5 percent. People are sort of flattish. |
| **K:** | You say you're in line, but you are doing only about $1 million a month. |
| **T:** | Six percent—I mean I am broadly, give or take. |

**K:**           Any idea of the percentage of winning trades?

**T:**           Yes. About 61 percent.

**K:**           How about your win/loss ratio?

**T:**           How do you calculate that?

**K:**           So, if you are making money 61 percent of the time, then ide-
                 ally you ought to be making more money when you are in win-
                 ning trades than you are losing in losing trades. You could
                 be up 61 percent of the time and still lose more in your los-
                 ing trades than you are making in your winning trades. It's
                 a good statistic. You need to pay a little more attention to
                 managing your losses and holding your winners longer. If you
                 have a good Sharpe ratio, that gives you a little more confi-
                 dence about getting bigger, particularly if you are up. Then you
                 have a little more of a cushion.

**T:**           A cushion is a good thing to have. It's much easier to trade
                 from in front of the news than to trade from behind. You are
                 trying to persuade yourself not to trade differently, but you
                 do.

**K:**           It's useful to know that your tendency is to size things incor-
                 rectly, not to get as big or use as much risk as is justifiable,
                 given your statistics. Typically, the risk manager comes in and
                 functions to remind you that you are down, and when you're
                 down it's a little more proactive. The key here is to convince
                 you to risk a bit more, particularly when your statistics justify
                 it. You are already pretty good at managing your losses.

As you heard, Theodore does well, but he could be up a whole lot more
if he sized his positions in line with his convictions. He is typical of ultra-
cautious traders who trade not to lose, rather than trade to win.

Did you know that out of all the Olympic gold medalists there are very
few who pursue another gold? Many medalists fail to recognize that they
have the capacity to win another. They remember the struggle. They remember the pain. They remember the effort it took to get to that winning
position, and they resign themselves to live with the memories of their
win instead of pursuing another. Theodore is experiencing something very
similar.

Earlier in his career, Theodore had some measure of trading success,
but with that success came some very personal struggles—particularly a
problem with anger that almost cost him his marriage. Now, years later,
Theodore has rebuilt his marriage and family life and is ready to revive his
trading career, but in his mind his trading success has been forever fused
with his inability to control his own emotions. He remembers the pain. He
remembers the effort, and he remembers the sacrifice. What he doesn't
remember is that his success did not have to lead to anger.

Sometimes those same successful athletes who fail to pursue another gold are troubled that they cannot reconstitute those long-lost feelings of vitality and loss of self that they experienced when they were first struggling to realize their vision. Their first medal was won by commitment to a dream and a willingness to work for it, without any certainty that it would be reached. And winning the medal was not what it was really all about. It was the *commitment* to win it in the face of uncertainty that made the experience rewarding.

Theodore doesn't realize that his wins were the result of a commitment to a goal and were not a result of his anger. He can re-create and even improve upon his trading success and learn how to deal with his emotional scars—if he will only commit to doing so.

## FAILING TO COMMIT

Ralph Waldo Emerson wrote about the dimension of yourself that flows effortlessly and without friction. When you make a commitment, you transcend your concerns, your self-image, and your need to appear in the world in a certain way. You begin to be in the world in a more authentic and powerful way, willing to "take the stand that you are the stand you take," without evidence or proof, merely because you have the courage to be who you are and to become what you are capable of becoming.

When you are committed, you are willing to speak the truth without fear of the consequences, and you bring all of your being into the present with the knowledge that this moment is an opportunity for you to express fully who you are. It is the first step toward creating your vision. You allow the present to unfold without knowing precisely *how* it will unfold. You are in a realm of uncertainty where nothing is known beforehand.

In terms of commitment, Theodore is failing miserably. He may argue that he is in fact succeeding in his personal commitments by not becoming too intensely involved with his trading career, but I believe that is not so. Because Theodore refuses to commit himself to his own dreams and goals, he is not being authentic with himself or his family. His fear of success, manifested in his inability to commit, could be costly not only in his career but also in his personal relationships, even if he doesn't recognize the danger.

In the following conversation, I specifically address Theodore's fears of succeeding and how his family life became intertwined with those fears.

**Kiev:** Have you considered that you may be afraid to succeed?
**Theodore:** I haven't given it any exhaustive thought. I have not been as successful as I initially expected to be in my career, but I am

very happy with my life. I have a lovely wife, and I have four kids that I adore. My family is my priority, but for the 10 hours a day that I am in this office my priority is doing this job.

**K:**    Do you think the way in which you pursue success is relevant to your children? Is trading at less than your best the kind of lesson you want to portray? If you're playing this game seriously, giving it your best, then they are going to know that. If you are not but telling them to give their best in their activities, then you are just giving them a mixed message, and they're going to know.

**T:**    Good point.

**K:**    So there is value in doing here what you are preaching. It's amazing what kids get that you never tell them. You had better become whatever you want them to be.

**T:**    You clearly have to present the right role model. I look at my two older children who are in high school, and I am humbled by what they achieve how extraordinarily proud I am of them. They are both very smart, but they both work in a way that I never even dreamed of working when I was their age. I am proud of their intellect, but I am more proud of their attitude. Given their attitude, I can't afford to slack off. I feel humbled by it, and I have to focus.

**K:**    You are so afraid of succeeding and the possibility of the problems that may arise with success that you are failing to put out the required effort. Is that right?

**T:**    The good thing about having failed certain things is that you're not afraid of it anymore. I used to be, but some things didn't work and I am still standing.

**K:**    Where did the judgment of yourself come from?

**T:**    The judgment was mine.

**K:**    You didn't grow up with it?

**T:**    No. I come from a family with no aspirations whatsoever. I grew up with a lot of unconditional love, which is good. But the bad thing is that nobody tried to motivate me to do more or be more. That's probably why I've married the women I have. I have been married twice. Both times I have married very driven women. At certain points in my career I have been profoundly driven. My present wife said that she would have no interest in being involved with a man who was driven.

**K:**    When your daughter decided to write a novel, did she say, "Is there some way I can write a novel?" or did she just start writing, and it became a novel?

**T:**    She basically said, "I am going to write a novel."

K: A vision is empowering, and it sounds like she understood it. When you grew up, nobody taught you that. You never learned the power of your own ideas or your own thoughts. You are saying that in the next five years this is what you want to do. It sounds doable. Another way of approaching this is to break down that five-year goal into smaller increments. What do you want to do in the next year, the next month, the next day, the next moment? There is no limit to how big your vision can be. You just have to continually tweak the process. You have to put it in numbers, but it's really understanding the power of the decision. Your daughter seemed to understand it instinctively. It is simply deciding to do something and then just doing it. The mechanics are secondary.

T: Awhile back I had a health scare. There was a period of four to five days where doctors were doing scans to determine if I might have cancer of the kidneys. During that time I began thinking about what I would want to accomplish if I knew that I didn't have much time left. I sat down and wrote down all the things I had to do and wanted to get done—in six months, one year, three years, five years, ten years. I was very focused but also very relaxed. Of course that was the perfect attitude to have. I thought I had no time or was reconciled that I was going to have some sort of shortening of my life.

K: Don't you think that exercise applies today?

T: Now I do because we are talking, and it just came back to me.

K: There is virtue in thinking like "this is it." That doesn't mean to stop working.

T: No, that was the interesting thing. When I wrote down what I was going to do, I was preparing to work. It was very clear that I was going to work and if I didn't like work so much, why else would I have written it?

K: You can create a program of who you truly want to be and then play to that. Your daughter did not think about who was going to buy her book before she wrote it. She just wanted to express herself. That's the whole game—finding your voice and expressing it. A goal gives you something to live by. Then you kind of work on it, finding ways of doing better and better.

T: I didn't have that during my earlier years. I just believed that I was the best trader there was. That was my target. That's all I needed. I was very competitive with other people, and I was just very intense. As my personal life became better,

I lost the intensity at work because I became a more relaxed person. I wasn't angry anymore. I don't want to become
the person I was when I was 20 to 30. I don't want to be that
angry person anymore. I like being this person.

**K:**          Do you think that in order to succeed at trading you have to
be angry?

**T:**          Yes, but I am beginning to realize now that I don't have to
be angry to be focused. I need to replace the fury with drive. I
can replace the anger with focused goals. During my twenties
and thirties I was operating from raw talent. There was no
training.

**K:**          Yes, but you had some kind of objective.

**T:**          Absolutely, just run faster than everybody else.

**K:**          You didn't think it through. Now, you have learned that you
can play the game in a much more centered, focused, and disciplined way. You can use your knowledge in terms of what
more you need.

To function in the realm of commitment Theodore must become comfortable functioning with uncertainty and learning from his past mistakes.
He must understand that the past does not have to be indicative of the future and that avoiding commitment does not lead to success in any realm
of life.

Slim Farman was a twentieth-century strongman who lifted 35-pound
sledgehammers while kneeling with his forearms flat on the ground. All he
used was the strength in his wrists. This interesting personality described
and clearly demonstrated how Theodore and other human beings are capable of achieving much more than they often believe.

Farman believed that our inhibitions and an inner governor keep us
from performing to our fullest capability. He cited the many cases where
ordinary people performed extraordinary feats in cases of dire emergency,
such a woman lifting a car off a pinned child or a severely injured man
walking miles to reach help.

"All this tells me that if what you are trying to achieve is more important than your own life (or if your life depends on it), then you can achieve
it," Farman once explained. "This is what I try to tell people. These are
things that shock your whole system so that you don't even have a chance
to think about the safety of it."

He continued: "If you want something bad enough, and you live it every day of your life, I don't think your size, your stature, or anything else
has anything to do with it. There is so much power in your body that is
only unachievable because you have a governor instilled in your brain that

shuts you off way before you reach your limits. If you can find a way to block out that 'governor' then you can find out how much power is in your body."

In addition to commitment, concentration, and focus, Farman explained that a lifelong desire to reach your goal is vital. That is how the governor is put out of commission.

When a trader finds himself stopped or, like Theodore, fails to reach his fullest potential, he should ask himself, "Why did I stop? Why did I stop putting forth the effort that was necessary to reach this goal?" Often he finds that there is no reason or that his reasoning is faulty. At that point, he has the option either to continue to trade in this restricted, unreasonable stance or to break through these self-limiting thoughts and move beyond his greatest imagining. Theodore can commit to a vision. He can live in terms of this vision. He can begin to tap into hidden and undetermined aspects of his potential, the extent of which may be even larger than what he previously thought.

## MOVING FORWARD

Like Theodore, most traders believe that they want to win. But do they really? If many of them examined their real thoughts, they would find that as long as they are a little bit ahead, they don't mind losing or not achieving their maximum potential.

Fear of success results in part from excessive concern with self-image and a reluctance to surrender to the next action. Many traders have been socialized in terms of such contradictory values as doing their best, looking good, and not losing. Few, if any, have been reared to do what it takes to produce results in line with specific objectives. More fearful of looking like losers than being motivated to succeed, they prefer to stay in their comfort zone and play not to lose. Theodore, and other traders who are experiencing this problem, must learn to recognize each event as a new opportunity.

If you are uncomfortable with success, you may unwittingly invite failure as you approach success. You may fail to set objectives, or you may function at less than your full capacity, totally avoiding the possibility of success or failure. Here fear of failure and fear of success coalesce. The prospect of success intensifies fear of failing and leads to a reduction in effort, increased distractibility, and the acceptance of a mental ceiling on your efforts, which serves as the rationalization for not maximizing your potential.

So, what should Theodore do? What can you do to move beyond your fear? Let's examine some basic steps you can take:

- Notice which obstacles frighten you most. For Theodore, it was the issue of anger management. For you it may be a particular type of trade or a particular amount of money. Identify what stumps you the most and throws you into a panic.
- Determine what advantages you are gaining from following your old routine of trading. Theodore felt secure. As long as he wasn't giving it his all, he reasoned he wouldn't become angry and therefore wouldn't jeopardize his relationships. What's your reasoning?
- Admit your need for help. Don't focus on being so much of a lone wolf or an individualist. When forced to verbalize his goals, Theodore had someone to hold him accountable.
- Get coaching from someone who has been exposed to the same obstacle and recovered or from a professional coach or mentor experienced in helping people overcome internal obstacles.
- Set stretch goals that are challenging and achievable.
- Commit to trading to win, to enjoying what you are doing, and to doing things on your terms.
- Decide what actions are needed to reach your objective, and take them.
- Visualize the future once you have reached your goal.

## Case Study in Recalling Positive Memories

As Theodore began to understand that success as a trader did not have to be permanently linked with the emotion of anger, he also began to recall some of his positive memories of trading. By learning to harness his emotions, set goals to strive for, and then recall the positive memories associated with success, he began to formulate a new plan for his trading career.

**Theodore:** I remembered yesterday some of the fun aspects of trading. I thought, "I need to keep myself in this 'fun' mode and not take things so seriously, because that leads to stress." That would be really helpful. I thought you might have good suggestions on how to stay in that mind-set.

**Kiev:** It's a visualization kind of thing. If you can remember what that experience was like and actually recall it before you even come in to work, you can get yourself into that mind-set. It's producing a state of mind.

**T:** That's what I want to do.

**K:**     The more you can visualize your past successes, the more you can get back into that state. Visualize and prepare for it. You may even look at using the past as a way of capturing and getting back into that mental state. You can also map out your plan for the day and start visualizing where you're going to start selling, where you're going to start buying, and so on, so that you're mentally preparing yourself. Keep formulating so that you have a plan. Then let reality dictate how your plan unfolds.

Theodore, like many traders, perceived that when you pursue your vision without any certainty and by relinquishing control, there is a freedom to be that will enable you to produce incredible results. When you are limited by the past, you will have less freedom and begin to be fearful.

In addition to more personal concerns such as Theodore's problem with anger, you may experience the added pressure of a past performance image and the expectations of others. You are also likely to be too focused on the outcome and not sufficiently trusting to allow yourself to engage in the step-by-step processes that are necessary for producing the result. You may focus too much on the past result or be too eager to get to the end result, so that you do not focus enough on the activities themselves.

Pursue what you can immediately in front of you, and you will reap positive results. If you focus on the outcome, your focus is in the wrong place. Focus on the actions you can take immediately before you, all the while keeping the end result in the recesses of your mind.

# CHAPTER 9

# Perfectionism and Paralysis

*M* *ackey was doing fine. In fact, compared to a lot of traders, he was doing quite well. But he was not as successful as he could be. Mackey's perfectionistic personality was undermining his efforts and actually leading him toward a path of mediocrity.*

*A problem solver by nature, Mackey was a dispassionate man who loved the process of learning. However, he tackled only the jobs that he was confident he could fix. In other words, he never strayed beyond his comfort zone. His constant need for accomplishment led him to avoid obstacles that he presupposed he could not overcome. Unfortunately, this unwillingness to venture beyond his comfort zone kept him safe but also powerless. Mackey had tamed his competitive spirit with his desire for security. When he failed to apply his abilities, he justified his actions as "cautiousness."*

*Mackey was not giving his all. He held himself back because of an innate desire to always be successful—to the degree that missing out on great success became acceptable as long as average success came with little failure. Mackey had to learn how to harness that inborn competitor, that innate learner, the adventurer that he had hidden so long.*

Looking at Mackey's statistics, I saw that he was up 63 percent of the time and had a W/L ratio of 1.41 with very low volatility of 3.73 percent and a Sharpe ratio of 4.71. His return on invested capital was 50 percent. He had no problem sizing positions. His maximum-sized position at one point was $19 million or 26 percent of buying power on the long side and $11 million or 16 percent of his buying power on the short side. He was relatively concentrated, with the average number of positions per day being 10 longs and 10 shorts. He made money in all holding periods.

The problem was that Mackey did not deploy as much capital as his statistics suggested he could. His return on invested capital was 50 percent, but his return on allocated capital was only 18 percent. With $75 million of buying power, his average gross market value (GMV) was only $27.6 million. Clearly, he needed to make a conscious effort to get bigger in his high-conviction ideas.

## THE PROBLEM

As I suggested in Chapter 4, some traders believe that in order to be successful they must be perfect. This is a false assumption, since it reduces the chances of learning from experience.

Perfectionistic traders are reluctant to get bigger. They don't want to leave their comfort zone. They won't trust their instincts that would propel them to move to the next step. These traders are inclined to obsess about potential problems and the attitudes, responses, and anticipated criticism of others. Such perfectionistic thoughts block their opportunities to do their very best.

For example, Mackey's concern about not losing and his fear of being hurt would not allow him to hold to a new concept of trading potential. He rationalized his behavior instead of increasing his risk. He hid these fears behind a curtain of caution. Mackey needed to stop covering up his hesitation in order to aim higher, to pursue his vision. Only by confronting his fear and accepting his mistakes as part of his humanity could Mackey join the masterful traders who view mistakes as learning opportunities.

## FINDING A SOLUTION

Often perfectionistic traders want to wait for every indicator to be perfect before they pull the trigger. They are afraid to enter the realm of uncertainty. They begin to romanticize the past and forget that they were once willing to take risks. The challenge, then, in working with perfectionistic traders is to help them to step out into the void—the gap between where they are and where they want to be—to do what works.

Mackey needed to accept responsibility for his vision by seeing how his responses to events colored the flow of events. By taking responsibility for his vision, Mackey could start making decisions about the direction in which he wanted things to go and begin to influence the outcome.

There are certain fundamental, rational, and pragmatic steps to maximize every trader's capacity to tap his full potential and become a super trader. As a first step, Mackey accepted the basic premise that he alone was responsible for his trading results. He began to understand that he had to take responsibility for what he saw in the market and for the trades he made based on that vision. This simple change of perspective to trade in the realm of action, purpose, and self-determination would begin to have an enormous effect on the way he trades.

## Case Study in Taking More Risks

The following conversation involves Mackey, Jackson (the risk manager), and me. We are attempting to encourage Mackey to use more capital. It is interesting to note that even the normally conservative risk manager is supporting the notion of increased risk based on Mackey's statistics and his ability to get bigger.

Again, Mackey's numbers at the time of our discussion were great: 45 percent return on average GMV, 4.71 Sharpe ratio, 63 percent winning trades, and a 1.31 slugging ratio (ratio of average P&L on winning trades to average P&L on losing trades). The familiar challenge with Mackey was capital usage. He averaged 37 percent capital usage for the year (average GMV of $27.6 million versus $75 million in buying power). Although low in absolute terms and well short of where he wanted to be, this was still a 70 percent improvement over the previous year, when he averaged $16 million in GMV. So, it was important to note that he was making progress. In this conversation Mackey begins to formulate and discuss his plan for increasing risk.

**Jackson:** The key thing that I look at is the percentage of winning trades. You make money on two out of three trades, and on those you make $1.30. That's a recipe for success no matter how you slice it. In a market that has been sort of flat this year, you are extracting alpha for both the long side and the short side. The biggest challenge is using more capital. You can do that in a number of ways. You can make positions larger, or you can trade more names. The reality is it probably requires a combination of both. Your stats tell me that in both the long and short sides you haven't been afraid to put on size when the conviction is there. You have averaged about 20 names in your portfolio, 10 long and 10 short. So, in terms of using more capital, can you put more positions on?

**Kiev:** Are there other issues involving Mackey's performance?

**J:** The other question is: Can you begin to take more than just the best ideas that come along only a couple of times a year and put them on for size? I have seen you put on size at times with more of the super-high-conviction ideas, but can you increase your size on the medium- to high-conviction ideas that are happening a lot more frequently?

**Mackey:** I agree 100 percent that I need to increase my size on the everyday stuff. You want me to be bigger. I am actually committed to it, and I have been trying to. The question is, what's the most effective way or the easiest way to get bigger? We need a prescription to follow, something like any idea starts at $3.5 million before we even do really deep research. Then, with conviction and a proprietary edge, it goes to $10 million. If it's a great idea, then it goes to $20 to $25 million.

**J:** In terms of a single position?

**M:** Yes. I have two analysts. I want them to have three to five types of these positions all the time.

**J:** The good ones will then be $10 million positions?

**M:** Well, $3.5 to $5 million would be the initial amount put on. The middle tier would be a range of about $10 million.

**J:** This year you were only $10 million when you knew it was a great idea. The only reason that the $20 million position was there was because it was a once-in-every-five-years kind of idea. This year if you just have a good idea, then $10 million is more the level. If you follow this logic and even stick with the average number of positions in the portfolio, then you're going to get bigger in a hurry.

**M:** I don't think that is such a big leap. It's just incrementally ticking up everything about 50 percent.

**J:** What about expanding in addition to this? Is there a plan to increase your coverage? Can you look at more more names and maybe have more stuff on the sheets?

**M:** I think our plan is to increase our coverage size a little bit more. I have the capacity and the place for it. I just need to be able to monetize this coverage list as it is.

**J:** You don't want to get bigger for bigger's sake. There is a risk of too much too fast.

**K:** I don't think that's going to be a problem with Mackey.

**J:**    It sounds like you have a good plan. I think you need to put a program in place, which is what you're talking about here. This year was clearly not a success in using more capital. The bottom line is you put more capital to work this year without any drop-off in performance. Clearly I am not worried about a drop-off in performance.

**M:**    What happens when people increase their capital? Obviously their net exposure is going to increase. I know it doesn't have to necessarily, but I think it probably does, and I know mine will. What would you say about how should I think about net exposure? My average net exposure this year is probably five to six million bucks.

**J:**    I don't recall your being on my radar screen for net exposure, but you're saying that could change as you put more capital to work. At $75 million I think you probably have a 30 percent net limit, which is standard. That gives you room to increase your shorts to $22.5 million. We could talk about increased use. If we find that happening more than a handful of times a year, we can reevaluate. Those are conversations I look forward to. My point is if you are sitting there running $20 to $25 million positions on any sort of reoccurring basis, even if it's once a month or every other month, then I think you have grown into your capital.

**M:**    I always welcome your pushing me to get bigger. My problem is that I have a lot of internal risk controls that I have developed, and I don't need to reinforce those as much as I need to let loose in those.

**J:**    I think I recognize that, and I hope that I have been pushing you toward getting more aggressive. Why don't I put monthly meetings in the calendar, and the three of us can get together again and review reports? At least we will get an indication on position sizing and the average number of positions, and we will go up from there.

You could hear the uneasiness in Mackey's voice when he talked about exposure. Nevertheless, he had enough confidence to ask Jackson to push him harder to expand his horizons and help him relax the restrictive controls he himself had put in place. With Jackson's reassurances, Mackey followed his plan and began using more capital. He recognized his perfectionism was holding him back and began to grasp the fact that he would not be the first trader to lose money on some of his positions.

A successful trader understands how his perspective influences events and consciously accepts responsibility for what happens in his life. When he does so, he no longer feels like the hapless victim of circumstances who is at the mercy of forces beyond his control. By accepting responsibility, he allows himself the power to produce trades in the direction of his goal.

Of course, this doesn't mean that there will be no effort or that the results will be guaranteed. But once traders decide to take responsibility for everything that happens in their trading, they liberate themselves from an inaccurate approach to the world and open themselves up to the possibility of tapping enormous suppressed resources.

## WHAT ABOUT YOU?

A perfectionist has difficulty recognizing that while winning is the object of the game, attachment to the end result will only be cumbersome. He may focus so much attention on victory that he loses sight of the pleasures of playing and ends up losing into the bargain. The self-induced pressure of thinking, "I've got to hit this one or else!" is never conducive to good performance. A desire to be number one can wind up being excessive.

By focusing on the end result, the perfectionist actually impedes his progress. He is often paralyzed by his fear of failure and afraid to take action, or he may become burdened by his methodology and unable to move forward to realize his vision.

Actually, the psychological pressure to win at all costs can make it impossible for a trader to enjoy his profession. This is especially true of perfectionists who typically become so preoccupied with results that they can't concentrate on or appreciate what is in front of them or even take the necessary steps to achieve their objectives.

Do you relate to Mackey or to the preceding description of a perfectionist? Do you have a problem with perfectionism or excessive caution? Consider the following:

- Are you too self-critical?
- Do you view your own efforts as insignificant or insufficient such that even when you are making progress you downgrade your own efforts and allow the voices from the past and the anticipated criticisms of others to lead you off your mark?
- Are you too caught up with a range of time-consuming activities that absorb energy and attention and distract you from taking responsibility for the full development of your interests?

- Do you characterize yourself as tentative or anxious?
- Are you easily scared out of trades when you are not sure of your assessment or the uniqueness of your perspective?

If you answered yes to the majority of the questions, then you too may be battling perfectionism. You have to learn to be comfortable with uncertainty and not make risk taking harder than it needs to be.

A master trader has zero investment in the intellectual assessment of the facts or the analysis of the data. All that matters to him is profitability. Can you adopt that attitude and bring it to your trading, even if it makes you uncomfortable at first? Can you identify those instances where you were reluctant to get into a trade because you lacked certainty, or got out of a trade before it fully developed? If so, why not practice observing your reservations and then figuratively balling them up and throwing them in an imaginary trash can? What you are left with is fact-based conviction without the inhibitions of perfectionism.

The master trader gets in on a trade with less certainty and stays in longer as the trade develops, thereby maximizing his opportunities for profit. He realizes that he can learn a lot simply by being in the trade and getting a feel for how it is going from the trading action itself.

Remember: Uncertainty and discomfort are inherent in the trading process. Your task as a perfectionist is to learn to deal with the emotions that accompany uncertainty and discomfort. True success will never occur if you continue to play it safe. In order to reach maximum profitability, you have to take risk—both with your money and with your ego. You have to move beyond your comfort zone.

Of course this is not going to be easy. For traders who have the type of personality that constantly wants to put the brakes on, this means learning to live with the possibility and reality of loss. How can you do that? First, create a plan. Mackey was smart enough to know that he couldn't just initiate change in a spur-of-the-moment type of way. He made a plan to incrementally increase his risk. He had parameters to follow, and that helped him feel a measure of security as he stepped into the unknown. Second, remember that if you risk nothing, you gain nothing. Everyone who has ever accomplished much has had to try and fail first. Therefore, prepare yourself for the inevitable. As you increase your risk, you are going to increase your chances of losing. That's okay. It's to be expected. So, prepare yourself for the inevitable. Understand that you will lose sometimes, and that while failing is disagreeable, complacency is worse.

In order for a perfectionist to become a successful trader (or even more successful than he already is), he must let go of his self-imposed limitations that prohibit appropriate risk taking. He must act even when the results aren't guaranteed.

## Understanding Risk Management

Although the successful trader wants his risks to be calculated, he knows that risks are necessary. For a trader to grow, he needs to learn how to take risks by measuring the risk/reward ratio. The goal is to trade when there is a favorable risk.

Mackey already had a good sense of risk management and only needed to learn how to increase risk, but many traders face a broader problem of not understanding risk management principles in general. The following are five suggestions for general risk management guidelines:

1. Build your portfolio and plan your trading strategy with some thought to the risk/reward profile of the trade. Have an expected price target where you will get out of the position and/or rethink your justification for continuing in the position, a stop-loss level where you will reduce your position by 50 percent, and a point where you will liquidate the position in line with good risk management principles. Develop a time frame regarding anticipated catalysts.

2. Build up some capacity for reading the markets and the sentiment component of trades, and don't rely entirely on fundamentals, especially if you aren't getting your timing right.

3. Be alert for short squeezes. Develop rules about reducing the size of your short position as it goes against you, recognizing that when this happens it becomes a more significant proportion of your entire portfolio—quite the opposite of what happens when your longs go against you and become a smaller proportion of your overall portfolio. The risks with shorts are geometric.

4. Capital preservation is the most important rule to observe. While you may be losing money testing your hypotheses, it is wise to know when you don't have an edge, can't read the crosscurrents in the market, and should reduce your capital at risk, waiting for better opportunities when your methodology gives you an edge.

5. Beware of macroeconomic theses if this is not your game. Don't make big macroeconomic bets on commodities and get away from your bottom-up approach to stock picking when things are getting tough. They will get tougher if you take shots.

It is wise to bear in mind that in today's volatile market being wrong will be more costly than in the past. Because of this, your ideas have to be better. You've got to make more money out of the ideas to offset the positions that don't work.

# CHAPTER 10

# Failing to Manage Risk

*F*rederick was up $10 million in February and approached his prof-
itability in a relaxed way. When he went up to $35 million by the
end of June, he raised his target to $50 million. But soon he be-
came too attached to the result and too uptight. He subsequently was flat
starting in July and was taken out of his game by family and medical
problems. He started thinking emotionally and trading like an amateur.
As the months went by, he became reluctant to cut his positions for fear
that they would move after he got out, which had happened to him before
on both the long side and the short side. Seller's remorse paralyzed him,
preventing him from cutting his losses and forcing him to frantically
trade ideas that he really didn't know, leading to additional losses.

To regain control and manage his risk, I suggested that Frederick
cut his portfolio to a number at which he could relax and not act so
frantically. While he was afraid of being a loser, I pointed out that it was
better to cut losses than stay in positions out of pride. Once he started
moving again and regained his confidence, he could pick up momentum.

He seemed relieved to be reassured that he could lower his expectations, take the pressure off himself, and then try to build momentum.
Within a few days he was down to using $46 million and was a bit
less stressed, but he was still angry with himself for being, as he said,
"a failure." He needed to remember that while the goal is important, he
shouldn't get so attached to it that he traded emotionally and swung for
the fences when he didn't have a good trade.

## RISK MANAGEMENT FOR A VISION

While risk taking can be stressful, managing risk should help reduce the stress. Successful risk management begins with a willingness to pledge oneself to living based on a future vision, without any certainty. You commit to a vision and create goals related to the vision, irrespective of the frightening inner voices that predict failure or ridicule. Thus you set a specific financial objective, then work backwards to develop a strategy consistent with that objective. You must focus on the implementation of this strategy without too much concern about reaching the goal.

### Case Study on the Battle between Fundamentals and Momentum

In the following dialogue, Frederick and Walter, one of his traders, talk with me about the role of risk management. Frederick is upset. His firm missed a rally because they didn't pay enough attention to the movement of the tape, preferring to stick with their own fundamentals.

**Kiev:**      How do you view the current market conditions?

**Frederick:** The market is completely irrational. The real point of contention is that we are out of sync with the tape. Everybody knows the exact same thing—that the numbers stink. Yet we have missed this rally entirely. Not only could we have been really long instead of short, but Walter keeps waiting for the market to come in. The stock prices are never low enough to buy. The conviction is not there when we see it.

**K:**        Maybe you ought to listen to him.

**F:**        (*to Walter*) I was talking about the frustration that we are both feeling about the tech tape and stuff. I thought maybe it would be good for you to talk about what you see.

**Walter:**   Ultimately, we are on the same page. We all want to make money, and we are very comfortable with that. Why I am frustrated is that the fundamentals are getting worse. I understand that people are looking for the turn for next year, and stocks are cheap. I honestly believe things are worsening.

**K:**        Then what's the explanation for the fact that the prices keep going up?

**W:**        I could give you multiple excuses about why the market is up. For instance, the energy tape has sold off.

**K:**  What is it that you haven't factored into your own assessment so that you would have been long rather than short?

**W:**  I have to see margins. The margins are already at their peak now. People are calling stocks expensive on peak margins.

**K:**  Are you saying it's very hard for you to take what you know?

**W:**  I follow fundamentals all the time. I am a rate-of-change guy.

**K:**  What do you have to do to become a profit-making guy? How difficult is that to do? Is it violating some internal kind of dynamic about the truth? What's uncomfortable about it?

**W:**  I wait until I see the whites of their eyes. Maybe I wait too long. Maybe I want to see a little bit more of a positive trend in fundamentals.

**K:**  Is it fair to say that somebody is making money in tech? You are not doing whatever that is that they happen to be doing. What's really going on?

**W:**  The few longs that I have, I do like what's going on. It's a product cycle. There are stories that I believe in, like in storage stock power integrations. We are getting an explosion in opticals now, because there are positive trends that will be happening next year. Semiconductors I just have a very hard time with, because they're cyclical.

**K:**  Are there other variables that you may need to consider?

**W:**  Maybe I am also afraid that I know the fundamentals are worsening.

**F:**  What do you think other guys know? Do you think you are the only guy who thinks the fundamentals are worsening? Do you have friends who are short and getting killed?

**W:**  Yes. I might be afraid because I have a tolerance for pain.

**F:**  That's when he decides he should be long.

**K:**  Too late; you got hurt once before. This is like post-traumatic stress. Once you have been traumatized you are a little gunshy. The virtue of the trading game is that you can move in and out. You almost have to separate what you do from what you know. You can't rely on what you know if it's contrary to what's happening.

**F:**  I think it's a very good point. I think if you are only going to use fundamentals, then you are missing a big part of the game. You are going to lose a lot more money on the short side because it has nothing to do with the fundamentals. It has to do with the other factors.

**K:**  If you are a smart analyst, your ego is a little bit involved. You want to be right for the right reasons. You say, "Well, I did the work and it really worked." Somehow or other you feel you are divesting yourself of your attachment to your analysis. If you don't have that attachment, you are just like any other gambler.

**F:** The goal is to make money. *Being right* is a relative term in my opinion.

**K:** If you like being right, you get attached to being right. It's very hard to let go of that. You get wedded to your assessments.

**F:** I am the member of the church of "what's working right now." That's what I worship. I will find something positive in a negative release if I see everything working. I will find something negative in a negative release if everybody hates them.

**K:** Maybe the answer is to say, "I have done the work. The fundamentals are getting bad. I want to be clear they are getting bad, but I acknowledge that the market is taking it this way." Conceivably, there may be more work that you can do to figure out a way of assessing that independently of your fundamentals.

**F:** We could say, "As of today it's not working, but we know when it does start to work the five names that would come in." I think we just have to keep in tune with the tape. We can't be afraid to short them when they are going down like they were in April. We can't be afraid to buy them when they are going up like they have been since April.

**K:** Isn't there a way of actually understanding what expectations are?

**F:** I think everybody knows things stink and they are getting worse. People are saying it's a quarter or two away from getting better.

**K:** How about other factors, such as oil?

**F:** This is a huge opportunity. Everybody wants to be early in these things. It's a fundamental game. I just think we are fighting it a lot, and that fight is really producing very shady results for our returns. We can't have that.

**W:** I have been trying to correct it. I have been meeting with a lot of companies over the past two weeks.

**K:** Companies are one thing, but what are some of the smart hedge fund guys doing?

**W:** Some people are just underinvested right now.

**K:** Do you know anybody who is playing this long?

**F:** Somebody is making money.

**K:** What will you do from this point on?

| F: | The most important thing you said was that there may be more work to do outside of the fundamentals about why it's going up. I don't hear that. Well, we have never had that discussion. How important is that? Maybe that's even more important than the current fundamentals. People can't buy what they don't see. To me that's an edge. You have got to buy what you don't see. By the time you see it you are late. You missed it. |
|---|---|
| K: | How are you holding up as you move forward? |
| F: | I need capital. It's tough. I think I have a great story. You are betting on 11 years, not one 12-month period. On an annual basis I have never had a down year. |
| K: | What do you say about managing risk? |
| F: | I have never lost money, and my annual liquidity really hurt me in talking to these investors. We were up 3 percent last month. They were all mad. I said, "You don't want to do this. Wait six months. This is the storm. We can have intelligent conversations when the sea is calmer. We have to get our money out. It's too dangerous." These investors really hurt themselves at the worst possible time. We messed up, too. We didn't hop on the gravy train; we were fighting it. |
| K: | When you look at your P&L, was most of your money made in your sector? |
| F: | Yeah, our sector actually has been pretty good this year. In fact, it has all ripped just in the last two months. One thing that we are going to do is run a little more leveraged, because I am not willing to sell my children at half price. It's a long-term game, demanding the work that is required. It's harder to implement than I thought. My style is not a successful style. I am trying to change because I believe that when things aren't successful they ultimately change. What we have to do is figure out whether that logic is correct. Is it sound? If it can work, then this is a great opportunity. I feel mad that everybody has had a big comeback. |

What I hear in this conversation is Frederick trying very hard to elbow aside his own vanity and his attachment to being right, and to maneuver his holdings differently simply to get back into the flow of the market. As smart as he is, it is difficult for him to watch others make the right moves for both right and wrong reasons. Gradually, he is letting go of his ego and agreeing that how others handle rallies and setbacks is not his problem. His only concern has to be making the necessary adjustments to a momentum that he can't control.

## THE PSYCHOLOGY OF RISK

Once again, let me state the rule of behavioral economics that stems from Nobel Prize winner Daniel Kahneman's studies as well as others: Most people are willing to accept risks in order to avoid losses but have a built-in tendency to avoid risks when seeking gain. My own observations during 40 years of psychiatric practice have led me to believe that most people lack the courage to take risks and to live their lives in the creative realm where there are no guarantees or certainties and where you can become only what you are willing to commit yourself to becoming.

Psychologically, most of us prefer comfort and safety to risk taking. Conditioned from early childhood, our lives are governed by various adaptive life principles that make our world more predictable and therefore less stressful. Unfortunately, those same life principles can also keep us locked into habitual routines at the cost of our creativity and vitality.

### Case Study: Being Realistic about Risk

Most traders are willing to hold on to losing positions in hopes that they will turn around, yet are more reluctant to add to winning positions. In short, a trader would take a greater risk in an effort not to lose $500 than he would to gain $500.

Consider Baker, who made most of his money in positions that he held for less than one week. That was where three-fourths of his trades were and where the bulk of his profit was. Unfortunately, the longer he held beyond that, the more he lost, and he was losing big. When he stayed in a trade for longer than six days, his average win/loss (W/L) ratio was less than 1, suggesting that he was losing more money in his losing trades than he was making in his winning trades.

After reviewing his statistics, Baker agreed that he needed to concentrate on his shorter-term trading where he seemed to have an edge. However, when we reviewed his stale and residual positions, he invariably had a rationalization for staying in his losing positions too long.

In order to combat this tendency, Baker decided to monitor his positions on a weekly basis and reassess the justification for remaining in longer-term positions and thus running the risk of increasing his losses, ever mindful that in the preceding year if he had gotten out of a lot of positions after one week, he would have made another $1 million.

Baker, like most traders, needed to remember that risk management means making realistic assessments of the market and his positions (gains as well as losses). Thus, risk management stands in contrast to being caught up in the rationalization and denial so readily triggered by events.

## THE IMPORTANCE OF SELF-ANALYSIS

Statistical studies of risk management have consistently demonstrated that most trading profits come from a small percentage of trades, approximately 3 to 10 percent, irrespective of the instrument traded. This points to the importance of maximizing profitability when the opportunity presents itself, which in itself is contrary to the natural impulse to hold on to losers and get out of winners.

Furthermore, since the most successful traders make more in their winning positions than they lose in their losing positions, they can be right in their stock selection as little as 40 percent of the time and still be profitable. This, too, points to the importance of being able, counterintuitively, to cut losses and maximize winning positions by getting bigger or holding longer.

A review of past performance is the first step for defining recurring, underlying patterns of behavior that may be contributing to trading success or failure. By understanding patterns in the markets, sectors, and companies, taking into account past experience, habitual distortions of perspective based on the nature of the market, and characteristic ways of handling stress, a trader can better manage his risk and reduce his stress.

### Case Study: Keeping Risk within Specific Parameters

Taylor was a methodical trader who was good at the kind of self-review that was needed in order to better manage risk and reduce stress. He was very detailed, used spreadsheets and price targets, and performed regular self-examinations of what went right and what went wrong. This information gave him clues about how he could improve.

For example, when he was down $1.5 million for the year, he began looking at his statistics and questioning why things weren't working as well as planned. He realized that he was having trouble timing the markets and that he had lost money whenever he tried to read market direction by trading the exchange-traded funds known as Spiders and Diamonds.

By developing a systematic way for reviewing his statistics, he began to observe what wasn't working. He found that he lacked a real cushion and was exposing himself to too much market risk. He also realized that he had been trying to recapture his losses in a few big bets, setting unrealistic monthly goals, and losing more than he was winning. He saw a pattern in his behavior: Several successive winning days were followed by significant losses because of 10 percent moves in fairly illiquid names that produced losses of $100,000 or more at a time.

"What have these self-evaluations accomplished?" I asked him.

"My expectations are more adaptive," he said. "I will have a lower tolerance for sticking with something I can't do. It's a humbling experience. I had a formulaic approach to this group that worked for many years. I now choose to look at it as a challenge. Let's adapt to the new environment. Part of the learning process is to be more skeptical when it is not working."

Specifically, Taylor decided not to trade merchant names. Rather, he traded relative price and fundamental valuation on 40 other stocks and was more nimble in shortening the duration of the portfolio. If something wasn't working, he got out and quickly adjusted to the news. Another possible solution was to partner up with someone who could discuss ideas with him and perhaps provide some insight into media and newspaper stocks as potential hedges. By improving his consistency and reducing large losses, he hoped to slowly build that cushion he had been lacking and to develop a more uniform track record.

"This environment calls for one to be malleable and agile," he said. His model didn't work. So, he changed the model. He overhauled his quantitative techniques and research in an attempt to adapt to the changing market environment. He now had submodels among groups of stocks that seemed to be more related to one another. He had additional tools to give him mispricings in a shorter time frame. The research was now focused on where he thought he could get leverage and not on trying to forecast earnings.

Taylor learned the value of self-correcting and aimed his trading proactively on making money, rather than on the avoidance of losing money. His new goal was to have a positive P&L by the end of the year, and he felt he was moving in that direction. He adjusted sizes and durations. Taylor's efforts to understand his former strategy, how it failed him, and what he needed to do to turn things around were major steps toward appropriate risk management and stress reduction.

Traders must consciously and continuously seek ways for mastering the natural inclination to avoid risk. Risk management is about taking deliberate action in the face of the uncertainty, unpredictability, and undetermined odds of the market, in the midst of continual and increasing stress. It requires that you stay with your hypotheses and discipline in a way that produces consistent results. This means trading on the basis of an accurate assessment of such catalysts as earnings, analyst upgrades, and company announcements; getting more aggressive with your winners; and getting out of high-risk ideas when you lack an analytical edge.

## ASKING THE RIGHT QUESTIONS

Risk taking is a willingness to act beyond the vicious circle of what you already know. What differentiates the winners from the losers is the capacity to stay on target and maintain an appropriate level of risk in the face of the stress responses and emotional reactivity triggered by the uncertainty of trading.

Managing your risk requires that you do what it takes in terms of sizing the position, measuring the probabilities of the upside reward against the downside risk, as well as getting out when things go against you and adding when they are going in your favor. Keep asking powerful questions about what more you need to do to produce the results or what may have dropped out of your trading approach when the results decline.

Challenge yourself with such questions as:

- What more do I need to know?
- What additional work can I do?
- What can I learn from my own emotional reactivity to the markets?
- How long should I hold a position?
- How fast should I get out?
- What kind of loss limit is tolerable?

The master trader gets out of a losing position unless he is absolutely certain from his fundamental analysis that the rumors forcing the price down are unfounded (which gives him the confidence to hold despite negative price action). Hope that a stock will turn around does not play a part in his calculations. Rather, he prefers to take the loss and buy the stock back when it returns and starts moving in a more positive direction.

### Case Studies in Assuming Risk

Less successful traders may be inclined to assume too much risk by swinging for the fences or may take on too little risk by using insufficient capital to produce specific results. They also are more likely to be distracted by their own self-doubts and inhibitions. They often have trouble committing to a specific result for fear that they will be disappointed or humiliated if they don't reach it.

For example, lack of a specific target was a chronic problem for one trader I know who invariably made $20,000 at the start of the trading day but whose gambling impulse to triple his winnings usually led him to lose everything he had made in poorly thought-out trades. This type of high-risk behavior—taking shots at trying to hit home runs—only left him flailing about with unsuccessful trades. Such behavior is particularly problematic in drawdown situations and often leads to even deeper drawdowns and eventual withdrawal from the markets when capital is depleted.

Another trader was so motivated by his fear of losing that he would get out of his positions when they went a half point against him. His losses were minimal, but he was equally reluctant to hold positions long enough when they were working. Therefore, he failed to benefit from the full range of the move. He was also reluctant to use all of his allocated capital and rarely, if ever, made significant amounts of profit.

What gives you the conviction to put more at risk and how you delineate the premise of the trade are two critical components to successful trading. To succeed, you must probe the reasoning behind why you are trading at your current size. In order to maximize your risk-taking ability you have to get bigger, and to do this you need to determine exactly what is getting in the way of your current risk taking.

## ASSESSING YOUR ATTITUDE TOWARD RISK

The following questions ask you to examine your own behavior in order to discover the sticking points in your attitude toward risk:

- What can I do to change my self-limiting habits and attitudes that are leading to repeated failures or insufficient success?
- If a habit, an attitude, or a life principle can't be changed, what new approaches to trading can I adopt that may transform my trading and empower me to realize my goals?
- What can I do to trade in a more risk-controlled way?

Failure in this business is behavioral and intellectual, and most traders need to keep learning more about the behavior of trading, the behavior of taking risk, the behavior necessary to be comfortable taking risk. Consider:

- What are you experiencing at the moment you are assessing the trade?
- What do you see?
- How do you see reality and take action in the face of uncertainty?

Less experienced traders who often get out of winning trades too soon have regrets about missing a move. Other traders take on too much risk because they are action junkies. These are some of the patterns that have to be identified and explained so that traders can modify their actions. Ask yourself these questions:

- How do you deal with ambivalence, uncertainty, and indecision?
- How do you avoid being trapped by overanalysis, regrets over previous losses, and other things that preoccupy you and keep you from trading in the present moment?
- What are the steps you need to take to make sure you get past your inhibitions and your perfectionism and can take the trade based on a workable idea?

Traders who are sincerely interested in managing their risks and maximizing their profits aren't afraid to ask these and other difficult questions.

## Case Study in Self-Analysis

Forrest was up $152,000 for the year in equity trading and an additional $12 million in foreign exchange hedges. He lost about $1.7 million in his short-term trading and made about $2.9 million from his longer-term trades. He tended to get bigger as high-conviction ideas went against him rather than adhering to risk management principles and cutting back on losing positions.

When reviewing these statistics, he began to consider whether he was cutting his losses too quickly and/or whether he lacked certain skills at short-term trading that he had already acquired at longer-term trading. To further investigate the issue, Forrest performed another analysis to look for significant patterns in 93 out of 444 trades where he had made money. He also developed more specific spreadsheets that indicated position size, volatility, catalysts, anticipated events, and entry/exit points to help him follow his positions in a more organized way so that he could tweak the portfolio.

From his self-analysis, he decided that he needed to increase his size in high-conviction ideas and get into fewer positions. He learned that it is better to get out of losing trades rather than staying in them with the hope that things will change and tries to remember that he can revisit a stock if it reverses and starts to improve.

Unlike Forrest, many traders are hesitant about performing this kind of self-analysis. They don't want to consider how they are creating problems in their trading and how much of their difficulty stems from the grip of their own past programming. They continue to act in a self-protective way, designed to preserve their image and to avoid certain kinds of stressful experiences. In doing this, they fail to see how much they are managing their emotions because of a need to appear in control and how this behavior generates more stress and keeps them from actually trading successfully.

The psychology of successful risk taking means taking a proactive rather than passive approach to the market and continually examining what it is you are doing that may be interfering with the trading process. Trading to win includes managing your trades with regard to good risk management principles, being more conscious of your own responses to the market, and observing how those responses influence your decision-making process.

## LOOKING FOR THE POSITIVE

Losses are inevitable. Moreover, as you increase your risk, your losses can increase exponentially. Knowing that it's part of the game doesn't make losing any easier. Unfortunately, the pain of loss can quickly lead to more loss if you become frustrated or depressed and allow your negative moods to affect your trading decisions.

Even in the face of loss, it is wise to look at what you did right. By giving yourself a mental pat on the back for even the smallest success, you can learn to feel a sense of achievement in the trading process and not just in the profit. And while it may not take the place of a big win, it will certainly feel better than beating yourself up. Additionally, if you look closely enough, you should be able to find something you did right even in the worst-case scenario.

### Case Study in Strengths and Weaknesses

Every trader should look for ways in which he can capitalize on his strengths and weaknesses. Unfortunately, some traders spend so much time concentrating on their areas of weakness that they wind up facing increased losses because they have neglected the superior aspects of their trading experience that could lead to wins.

For example, Nash was concerned about his stock-picking and risk-taking abilities. After reviewing his entry and exit positions, I found that he frequently held on to positions even after bad news had come out, often giving back the profits he had made. He was trading defensively as opposed to proactively and was afraid of losing money. This defensiveness showed up in a number of losses in stub ends where he held on to 10,000 shares of a position in order to watch it and ended up losing several hundred thousand dollars as the stocks moved against him when he wasn't paying attention to news events.

Nash isn't necessarily a bad trader. In fact, he has a gift for using technicals and keeping good notes about his plans for entry and exit points. He just hadn't been using any of that information. In fact, he stopped using his technicals and had become too reliant on the analytical orientation of other traders. He agreed that it was critical to get back to his own game.

After giving him a few days, I once again reviewed Nash's trading. He had returned to using his technicals and keeping good notes about his plans for entry and exit. As he did this, he was gaining more confidence and starting to make some money. He realized that he should have stayed with his original trading game based on chart review and preparation and factored in the analytics to that approach, rather than change his style.

There is almost always a positive side to consider; doing so can only help decrease your stress and increase your confidence. To be a successful trader you have to learn not to allow every loss to send you into a panic. By viewing each situation in a calm and objective manner, you are more likely to make wise decisions.

## RELAXATION AND RISK

While most people would say that the two words are opposites, there can be a place in which risk and relaxation meet—at least to some degree. If you are in the middle of a big risk-taking endeavor, you should not be so relaxed that you become cavalier, but you can find a sense of calm that will serve to help manage your risk more effectively. In fact, in order to ensure that your stress levels do not undermine your risk-taking efforts, it is imperative to do whatever you can to help stay calm, even in the midst of crisis.

You may find relaxation by keeping a tidy, organized workspace or listening to relaxing music. The options are endless (and I will discuss some in more detail later in this book). If, for example, being at the ocean is a relaxing experience for you, download or bring a CD of ocean sounds to listen to or pictures from your beachside vacation to place on your desk. When you are feeling stressed, cue the CD or download and spend a couple of moments breathing deeply and looking at your photos. For more details, check out the exercises in Chapter 14.

While you may already know what helps you to calm down, you may not make the most of those activities or exercises on a daily basis, or even consider how such things could benefit your trading experiences.

In addition to the stress associated with risk taking, there are always outside sources of stress that you may bring into the office—relationship issues, personal finance problems, health concerns, or everyday stresses like the traffic you encountered on the way to work. As hard as it is to do, it is vital that you learn to drop those concerns once you open your office door.

I heard about a man who used to walk up to a tree in his yard every evening before entering the house. He would stand there with his hands on the tree for a minute and then go in. Finally, a curious neighbor asked him what he was doing. He explained that he had developed a bad habit of taking his work frustrations out on his family. To avoid that problem he began "unloading" his problems onto the tree. By taking a minute to "hang" his work problems outside the house, he helped clear his mind and de-stress before entering his home to spend the evening with his family. He said he could always pick the problems back up the next morning before he headed to work. I would suggest traders could borrow this sort of action both at home and at work.

The markets provide enough stress for the day. Try not to bring any more with you. Mentally make an effort to leave your personal problems outside the office door so that you can focus on your trading strategy and risk management principles.

Last but not least is the physical component to any activity, including risk management. Don't forget that taking care of your body will help relieve stress in general. Eat right, exercise, and get the proper amount of sleep. If you go to a gym regularly, analyze what is the right time to exercise. Does your gym workout give you a jolt of energy before your day begins? Or are you the type who gets exhausted and thus it might be smarter to work out at the end of your workday? Our bodies are simply not hardwired to deal with stress when we are not feeling well and definitely not when we are tired. It is difficult to adhere to risk management principles and to not give in to emotional responses when you are exhausted or physically distracted.

## TAKING RESPONSIBILITY

When traders know how to manage risk, they will not eliminate stress, but they will be able to trade with confidence. A successful trader does not and cannot focus solely on the wins. If he does, he will never have the persistence to overcome the stress of losses. Stress will lead to a distorted view, and a distorted view of the markets, your strategy, your losses, or your wins will only lead to more mistakes. When a trader can only concentrate on winning, his demeanor will be not be calm or focused. By following a trading strategy, expecting occasional losses, and accepting them when they come, traders can be more consistent and therefore more likely to win in the end.

In reality, if you are not achieving your trading objectives, it is not due to circumstances or bad luck or even the stressful market conditions. It is because you are creating the very reality that you consciously or subconsciously expect. You may even work harder and harder without producing a new result, convincing yourself along the way that you are doing the right thing and that the lack of results is due to circumstances. If you begin to explore these issues, you will soon discover that what is missing is a commitment to a meaningful and concrete trading objective and a sense of responsibility for the outcome.

## Case Study in Adjusting Strategy

Consider Russell and Jorge, two long-term, value-oriented hedge fund managers with a team of four analysts who covered health-care, finance, technology, media/telecom, and retail/consumer sectors. They had been driven by their long-term strategy with an average holding of three to six months and a basic discomfort about shorting stocks. When they made money shorting they covered fast, fearing that they would lose their profits.

"We don't have the stomach to hold on to our shorts," they said.

They were running about 10 percent net long and consciously avoided market timing. They had not been able to trade technology in the prior few years because of their reluctance to short stocks, the fact that they were not market timers, and their lack of a sense of the trading flow. As a result, they had not made much money.

They started to tweak their strategy by trading Spiders instead of shorts, but were more invested in maintaining a consistency in their approach than in profitability and were not willing to make significant adjustments in their strategy to impact their P&L. They were afraid if they changed their market exposure (which they believed was critical for success) they would mess up their strategy and lose more money in the end. In fact, they said their strategy did not work in certain environments (e.g., bear markets). They didn't like to trade the volatility and were scared by big drawdowns. Moreover, they lacked a trading infrastructure. Their principle mantra was preservation of capital, and they prided themselves on being risk-averse.

After examining some of their statistics, I discovered that the team had an abysmal record in all of their accounts. They were down about $19 million for the year. In looking at their risk profile, it was clear that they had more losing days than winning days and that they lost more money on their losing days than they made on their winning days. As they said, they were both risk-averse and good risk managers insofar as they reduced their capital exposure as they went into drawdown, which was a good sign.

Basically, even though the market had been going down, they remained net long throughout the year. So, the question continued to be whether they could change their stripes enough to adapt to a more balanced kind of portfolio and take a more opportunistic rather than a long-term value approach.

In order to have the greatest chance at success, you have to look for those trades that have the best odds. This requires perseverance, hard work, and patience. You have to learn to decipher the difference between what a stock is now and where it will be in the future. In order to do this, you need to learn how to consider the expectations that are built into the process, how to get bigger and stay longer in the winners, and how to get out of the losers faster. Learning to manage your risk, and therefore your profit potential, is a matter of consciously deciding what must be done to achieve your objectives and then doing what is necessary to accomplish the task. A by-product of learning to manage your risks will be a decrease in your stress levels.

# CHAPTER 11

# Failure to Dig Deeper

*E*verett was in a *"trading funk where nothing worked."* He *"couldn't get it right"* and had lost confidence in his day-to-day decision-making ability. Volatility expanded rapidly during a four-week span, and he didn't expect the numbers to be as bad as they turned out to be. So, he didn't take his positions down. He lost $4 million. The trades were crowded; he should have been more aggressive in hedging and he should have reduced the size of his positions. He wasn't big enough in the unwind side and thought he had hedged his positions reasonably. Too many of his hedges were correlated to the market direction, and he should have been two to three times bigger on the unwind side. He knew he could be wiped out but misperceived the timing.

When he examined the situation further, he realized that he was in some trades that were relatively new for him and he increased his risk by adding to trades that turned out to be different ways of expressing the same bet. Unfortunately, his risk systems weren't really in place. He apparently also took his eye off the ball by getting involved in so many unfamiliar trades and assuming that the macro trades were good.

In fact, Everett's problems had a lot to do with his method of information gathering and the stress he was experiencing as a result of his recent losses. In order to get back on track, Everett had to better differentiate the so-called noise from the information available to him and to become more active in the management of his positions. He had to trade fewer strategies, reduce the size of his relative value trades, become more active in the macro sphere, and become more of a contrarian. He also needed to achieve better risk control by getting out of positions that

*weren't working. He needed to keep moving and not become paralyzed by
the price action.*

Everett is far from being the only trader with issues about information gathering. The process can be stressful, especially for nonanalytical
types. As we discussed earlier in the book, some people are naturally
wired to be impulsive or to take extreme risks with insufficient information or thoughtfulness. For these traders, the practice of digging deeper
can seem mundane and trigger a variety of anxiety responses. Beyond this,
their aversion to analysis and a lack of confidence in their intellectual
prowess hamper some of those traders, especially at times when things
aren't working.

Conversely, traders who become too absorbed with information gathering can also create added stress for themselves. They spend too much
time digging in and too little time actually placing the bet. Traders who are
obsessed with getting the whole picture right can increase their levels of
stress when they gain too much information to adequately process it or use
it, or when they postpone action in order to gain more information.

Of course, some traders may come into the process of information
gathering already besieged by anxiety, and this anxiety can actually interfere with how they gather and perceive data. As a result they lack the
psychological energy to think strategically and to look for original ways of
examining the material they collect. For example, they may fail to seek out
innovative perspectives that might give them an angle on company change.
Stress-ridden traders forget to keep triangulating information—checking
with a variety of sources to prove or disprove a theory, as well as double-
checking data to ensure accurate stock judgment.

Other anxious traders lack the patience to gather data points from a variety of perspectives so as to form their own conclusions or make their own
decisions. Instead, they may be too quick to act on inadequate information
and tend to believe in their ideas rather than developing a skeptical or ag-
nostic view of their analyses. Moreover, they may become too attached to
ideas and inclined to be unwilling to be flexible or adaptable in the face of
new information and perspectives.

An almost phobic avoidance of stress may keep other traders from
stretching to obtain more information or from asking difficult questions,
because they are fearful of appearing foolish or wrong. Neglecting information gathering can only lead to more losses, which subsequently only
lead to more stress.

Actually, the process of information gathering can be a way of helping
reduce anxiety. When a trader is as prepared as he possibly can be and is
trading on the basis of reliable information or research, his levels of anxiety
should be less than if he were taking a shot in the dark.

## DISCERNING THE IMPORTANCE OF DATA ANALYSIS

To take increased risk in the marketplace requires a combination of understanding the fundamentals and having the courage to trade your convictions. Trading bigger requires more data gathering and processing so as to produce results.

### Four Steps to Taking Bigger Risks

1. Create an information edge so that you are ahead of the curve.
2. Have a thesis that you can support with data.
3. Assess the sources of the data.
4. Trade on the basis of this data against others in the marketplace.

The trader who understands risk will pay attention to corporate numbers and guidance and will try to analyze the relevance of these numbers to where the company stands relative to its major competitors. He is also able to differentiate between companies and does not simply trade noise or daily movement.

The best traders focus on the company balance sheet, earnings reports, and an assessment of the growth prospects of the company. They also compare the company on a relative valuation basis to other companies in the same space. They consider the state of the economy and any significant macroeconomic variables, such as Federal Reserve interest rate cuts, the cost of energy, and the cost of doing business, and try to assess the nature of the market at the time.

To improve your data, ask yourself: Is this a market that is trading on fundamentals, or is it trading on macroeconomic variables and market sentiment? Then try to get a handle on relevant short-term catalysts—fresh earnings news, changes in top executives, new technology, for example—that may influence the market's perception of the value of a stock. Once you take these steps, you can try to make a calculated bet on the impact this data will have on the price of the stock.

Master traders are likely to factor all these things against their past experience in trading the stock, and may buy or sell some of the stock to get a feel as to how the stock is trading. Here they are also interested in the price action and what that tells them about the supply and demand characteristics of the stock—how it is trading based on an interest in buying or selling it among other investors and traders.

With all this data analysis, they then try to determine the risk/reward profile of a particular trade in terms of its upside versus the downside of the trade. To the extent that it fits within their parameters (say a 3:1 risk/reward ratio) they enter into the trade, all the time being careful to balance the trade in terms of their net long or short exposure. Oftentimes they hedge a bet by making a comparable trade in the opposite direction or by holding options, which they use to leverage their bet and protect their downside risk.

## Case Studies in Lowering Stress by Gathering Data

Thomas was a trader who understood the benefits of data gathering in order to lower stress. In fact, he had developed a very definite methodology for sourcing short ideas. He maintained a list of 50 critical questions based on his assessment of thousands of companies. He continually generated additional questions to ask of those companies that showed a divergence between rising earnings and declining cash flows (a signal that the company was having major problems).

One of the best practices Thomas followed was to ask his brokers to ask their analysts to answer a list of questions each week. His hope was that this screen would yield him five recommendations from which to extract at least one good short idea per week. With that one idea he worked on one company a day, hoping for a year-end return of 25 percent. With a detailed plan of action as well as digging deeply into a limited number of companies, Thomas optimized his opportunities and helped eliminate or at least reduce unnecessary stress.

While many traders recognize the need for information gathering, others tend toward complacency.

Such was the case for Grant's large hedge fund in London. After an intensive trading seminar, he began to realize the need for his analysts to dig deeper than they were actually doing. As the chief investment officer, he realized he had to do something. At the same time, he recognized that motivation in this area was not going to be easy to muster. Here he provides a good description of the kind of resistance that is often encountered when challenging traders to gather more information.

"After our seminar," Grant said, "I had another off-site meeting with my team of analysts and traders. I talked about how we might do research better and also discussed what attribution might do for us. I challenged them in a deliberately direct and uncomfortable way to raise their game. I told them that complacency would destroy us (and that meant all of us)."

He continued, "My sense is that this was the start of a long and painful journey for most of them. There is a coziness and a latitude here that has enabled a lot of idiosyncratic people to do their own thing with limited amounts of what might be regarded as either deep or systematic analysis. There is an understandable reluctance to change from the known to the unknown (in terms of higher-conviction investing). I believe that the prevailing sentiment has been that we just need more volatility and our returns will go up again and therefore we do not need to change. As a result of our off-site meeting, this theory has been challenged. A lot of evidence undermined this view and clearly hit home."

Grant concluded: "I think we are at the stage equivalent to when you get someone to admit they need to lose weight, but they are secretly hoping you will leave the room so they can continue to raid the cookie jar. Our traders know it is bad for them, but we are still some way from getting them to change their habits. I left all of them with a sheet for possible process improvements. I will follow up with each team to see what they are considering, but I suspect that the initial response will be one of ostensible apathy and denial despite the epiphany that they had at the off-site."

Despite the obstacles, managers and individual traders would do well to follow Grant's example and pursue a strategy of digging deeper. A step-by-step method of helping traders look for more and better information may be painful at first to initiate but will prove beneficial in the long haul.

## TOO MUCH OR NOT ENOUGH?

How much data do traders need to rely upon to take action? In a society bombarded with information from a myriad of sources, a trader has to determine what is relevant and what is unnecessary.

### Case Studies in Optimizing Data

The goal of Michael's team was $4 million a month, a figure that was reverse engineered from quarterly goals since the team members built their portfolio around intermediate-term ideas. But the reason they were not getting to their numbers was in part a reluctance to size their positions commensurate with their objectives because they were unfamiliar with some of the sectors. Their lack of information left them in the dark; they did not have the confidence needed to build up these sectors. The entire team needed to be encouraged to dig deeper and press harder when they believed in the profitability of positions they recommended.

Jake knew the amount of work that was needed but wanted to cover as many companies as possible to create a good impression. He was nervous about venturing deeper into the realm of uncertainty, where original thought was required. So he stuck to plain-vanilla data points that didn't give him much conviction.

A lot of traders discover that too much information can be equally stifling, since it may take so much time to collect. Overwhelmed, such traders grow paralyzed and miss key trades. In effect, the opportunity often passes while the trader is still thinking about the best action to take.

Consider Ken, a trader who made about $800,000 one month but was finding it hard to get a handle on the markets. He was mostly balanced, with a slightly long bias, although he felt more comfortable being short, given the weakness in fundamentals.

Ken was starting to suffer from information overload because he was covering more than 100 companies. He was also trading in and out of positions fairly frequently, cutting his losses rapidly and unfortunately cutting his gains too rapidly.

I suggested that he might try to narrow his focus a bit and concentrate on those portions of his portfolio where he had the greatest edge. He was also planning to hire a senior analyst who could help with the screening and organization of some of the data he was gathering.

So, there is an optimal amount of data and a time frame for determining what action to take. If you are trading in a short-term time frame, you don't always need to dig as deeply into the fundamentals of the company and can make use of such short-term catalysts as conferences, road shows, earnings announcements, new product announcements, and the like to provide a rationale for a short-term trade. If you are a short-term, catalyst-driven trader, you have to pay attention to the daily fluctuations.

Long-term value traders, whose actions are governed by fundamentals, usually will take a more relaxed, longer-term approach to the daily fluctuations. This is true even though over time there are far more variables that can influence the price of a stock and contribute to long-term risk. For the longer-term trade, accounting issues, structural issues, and other fundamentals about the company are more critical. In either instance—short-term or long-term—it is critical to consider the underlying business and ask the right questions.

## GATHERING THE INFORMATION

There are some practical ways of sorting through the myriad amounts of data you may encounter. Data points are best considered relative to how they relate to specific trading decisions. Research either should make a trade look promising or should discourage you from taking action. A 1-2-3 rating system is one way to help you keep tabs on the information you are gathering and the trades that the information represents. In this case, you would rank your trades as follows:

1. Number 1 trades look like they will move up or down in the next day or two. They are trades that are backed with a lot of conviction and a short-term horizon.
2. Number 2 trades have a catalyst on the horizon, but the time frame remains unclear. Although you don't want to wait to buy or sell until the idea is a number 1, you also don't want to get too big in a number 2.
3. Number 3 trades are considered educated bets. You may not necessarily have a shocking insight, but you feel the bet is safe on a risk-adjusted basis. Number 3 trades are often used as sources of funds for number 1 or number 2 ideas.

This system is not necessarily a model for everyone to follow. But such a system is of value as a general example of how you can devise data guidelines or rules that complement your style and help you organize and sort the vast amount of data you are processing so that you can use it most effectively.

What follows is a list of questions and comments that you may want to consider when reviewing data and determining its relevance on any given trade.

- How long will this information (an earnings announcement, a change in the basic structure of the business, a significant conference or meeting) be relevant for trading this stock? Be able to state your case in a simple manner that anyone can understand.
- If you have doubts, look at the data again. Has anything changed? Is further research required?
- Remember that stocks are volatile and may fluctuate in response to events in the company, in the sector, and in the marketplace for short or longer periods of time and then revert back to the mean. Do you want to trade the intraday volatility for short-term profits? Are you holding the stock for a bigger gain over a longer period? Is your information and assessment relevant irrespective of the short-term movement in the stock?
- Consider the facts. If a stock is declining in price, yet the business is still healthy, it may still be worth holding that stock or buying more depending on your risk profile and your targets. Always weigh the information against the risk/reward profile of your decision to buy or sell a stock. Filter out the noise and keep on learning more about the

company and the reasons why it may be trading the way it is. Know as much as you can about the companies you are trading and the factors influencing movements in each company so that you can ride out fluctuations in the stock price.

Professional and even amateur traders can manage their risk and lower their stress in a controlled way by searching for relevant short-term events or catalysts that are likely to have an impact on the short-term movement of stocks. This is even more important than looking for hot tips.

## Case Study on Interpreting Data

Terry was a struggling trader who was finally starting to have a few profitable days. He did the fundamental work, and then his stocks got hit with rumors that turned his positions upside down and took away the small amount of profit he had made. He was trying to trade the trading ranges of his stocks, and, as an execution trader, he hoped to get off the desk so he could do more work. Still, he needed to learn how to wait for the catalyst and not get caught up in positions that became distractions until they worked; those distractions frequently took him out of the game.

Catalysts are incremental news events or data points that can move stock prices in the short term. Traders who are trying to take on more risk by reducing the amount of time they hold positions would do well to home in on these things to increase their edge.

There is also another level of analysis required beyond what is obtained from the Street. Trading in terms of the larger objective, you are looking for an incremental advantage in analysis that you will get if you are willing to play beyond the constraints of the numbers. While you are gathering as much data as you can about the company from company reports, conference calls, and the Internet, start listening carefully for subtleties from the reports of those close to the seat of power, many of whom can be heard on national television or at shareholders meetings.

Here, too, it becomes important to listen with the third ear and to read between the lines. Sometimes the most useful data is what is *not* being said. Body language and demeanor may suggest discomfort. Company officials might look as though they are hiding something. Traders need to be able to interpret and use this kind of hidden data when making trading assessments and develop a variant perception.

## Case Study on Variant Perception

Irwin was a successful trader, objective and levelheaded. He understood the context and the analysis. He questioned all premises and tried to understand which were valid and which were not. He did a probability analysis based on the risk/reward trade-off so as to increase his edge when entering a trade. The same analysis helped him decide when to pull out and take profits. Such information helped him to remain emotionally balanced so that he never approached anything from a point of weakness. He continually made assessments of what was real and what was not based on the facts and perceptions. If the data suggested that something was not real, Irwin considered how long the world would perceive it as real.

He was very comfortable with the idea of holding positions long-term (rather than trading around the positions) and working on some additional companies while maintaining an 800,000-share position in XYZ Corporation and waiting for the catalysts.

Critical to Irwin's process was the idea of finding the variant perception. He dug for information and believed that the issue for him was to find the big ideas and put unlimited amounts of capital to work on these big ideas, not to think about how much capital he needed to use. This intensive scouring process often yielded perspective on companies that might ripen in the future. Therefore, he was getting value from his efforts even when there were no near-term opportunities in some of the companies he was studying.

There are many resourceful ways of finding out about a company and how it is doing relative to its competitors and relative to its past. Whether reading between the lines or evaluating the truth of a rumor, it is important to acquire as much data as one can in order to make an educated prediction and to take the appropriate action—whether to buy into the rumor to make a quick hit or to hold off for more likely opportunities. This kind of work enhances the capacity to take measured risks.

In effect, to take on more risk without more stress, experienced traders need to dig deeper and deeper in understanding company fundamentals, technical indicators, and other information—separating market movement from basic fundamentals and taking measured bets based more on their understanding of the companies themselves than on market action alone.

## REDUCING STRESS

Even if you find information gathering stressful, remember that involving yourself in the here and now of the process will enable you to intensify the amount of effort and energy you give to a task without experiencing the fear and anxiety that come from focusing too much on the long-range outcome. While a goal sets the direction and provides a motivating force, only

## How to Convert Information into Improved Trading Performance

### Analyzing Trades Historically

Look at your five biggest winners and your five biggest losers. Compare the overall performance of those trades with the conviction levels that you prerecorded. See which ideas were above conviction and which were below. Take note of whether any comparisons can be made between unanticipated higher-performing and lower-performing trades. Ask yourself if there is a pattern that you have not been seeing.

### Analyzing Trading Performance

Ask questions to determine what kind of effort you are putting into new trading ideas. Consider where you have or have not made money. Are you digging in deep enough to find good ideas? How much time are you spending on each trade? Categorize different types of trades: convergence trades, earnings trades, data point trades, and informational trades, for example. Set different standards for different types of trades. Decide what information you need for each type of trade and how much time you feel should be spent on each one. Then, when you have an idea in that category, you can more easily evaluate it based on the standards you have put in place.

### Risk Metrics

If in your self-analysis you find that you are getting and implementing good ideas but still not making a lot of money, you may want to initiate an automated trading system. An automated system will force you to use more capital and help you get a clearer picture of your actions. The system can be arranged to meet your own parameters, or you can use predetermined parameters.

involvement in the here and now enables you to bring all of your resources to bear on your performance.

The more data you have, the more positive you can be about decisions, but that doesn't necessarily mean you are going to make better decisions. Commitment to the goal means acting from it without any guarantee of success, but with the same kind of enthusiasm you'd feel if you believed there was no chance of failure. Focus on *efforts*, not on results.

Ultimately, you will discover that in trading, as in life, success grows organically by living from the perspective of the goal without fear of failure.

The key to all of this is to be able to live in the present, to see every situation as an opportunity to hit a home run, to give it your best shot, and to keep focusing on immediate targets relating to the broader objective.

While you might not be comfortable no matter how much information you have, the importance of understanding the fundamentals in order to assess the real risk inherent in a trade is a critical aspect of managing risk. You need to increase the analytical edge that you have about a company so that you can properly size your position and make a directional bet. Once you have made these assessments, you also need to understand your own psychology and how it is being factored into your trading. Differences in beliefs and attitudes play a significant role in how you perceive the opportunities before you.

# CHAPTER 12

# Failures in Shorting

*F*elix had been experiencing the pain of holding short positions as they went up against him. This was a reasonably good strategy, especially when he had an informational edge. Unfortunately, anticipating the pain of a short squeeze was too great for him. As soon as a stock reversed direction and started going down (which was what he was playing for), he got panicky and got out of the position too quickly. In his anxiety about preventing the reactivation of the stress of a short squeeze, he failed to stay with the position as the value kept dropping. He therefore missed out on a large part of his potential profit.

Expecting that a specific stock is going to go lower in price is one of the most stressful types of trades, even for those who are good at short strategies. Traders like Felix need to learn how to handle the stress of shorting so that they will be better equipped to stay in the short as it comes down, maximizing their profit.

The ability to short stocks, which takes a very high level of conviction to execute, is an art form in its own right, and the act of short selling is not mastered by many. Finding short ideas is very difficult and takes a fair amount of stress tolerance. The market tends to go up. Most people and companies are apt to be optimistic. It takes very strong character traits to select shorts and then stick with them in the face of everyone else's optimism about the company or the economy.

## RELUCTANCE TO SHORT STOCKS

Due to the added stress of shorting and the increased need for appropriate data, many traders don't short as much as they could to increase their profits in situations where they have gathered relevant information related to the structural weaknesses of a company. Often traders lack the patience to do the work and discover when a company is likely to fold or decline in value. Even when they short stocks as a hedge against their longs, they often do so without having done the requisite research.

### Case Study: The Difficulty of Shorting

Dalton was a trader who preferred to go long and thought he would make more profit on the long side than on the short side. Even when the market was going down, he was not looking for shorts and therefore couldn't maximize his performance.

| | |
|---|---|
| **Kiev:** | Are you mostly long or short? |
| **Dalton:** | I am net flat. |
| **K:** | It looks like people who are short are doing pretty well. |
| **D:** | They're doing great. I try to make money on the long side. When the market goes down on the long side, I try to hedge it out. I usually short more of a hedge in a primary way. |
| **K:** | What's the reason for that? |
| **D:** | I think that a lot of hedge funds are bearish, and that's why I am trading hedged, but I still think you can make 10 times your money on the long side. You can only make one times your money on the short side. If the stock goes from 10 to zero, you have made 100 percent. If the stock goes from 10 to 100, you have made 1,000 percent. |
| **K:** | I understand that in principle, but does that contradict the direction of the market and the notion that if you were reading just the market you would be trading on the short side? |
| **D:** | I am keeping it flat. If the market goes up, I don't make a lot of money. If it goes down, I don't make a lot of money. I am just going to wait for things that I know well. |
| **K:** | Have you ever considered the idea of setting a target and letting the target govern your strategy? Have you ever considered asking yourself what you need to do to reach your target? Under these circumstances, where things are going down, you might have to shift gears a little bit. |
| **D:** | No, I have certainly not done that. |

**K:**      If you were trading just in terms of the way in which the market is going, would you shift a little more toward the short side?

**D:**      Yes, but I still think we would be down some.

**K:**      I am not here to tell you how to trade. I am just challenging the psychology of it.

**D:**      As I look at the market, I have gotten smaller, less concentrated on some of my longs. Why don't I just take a shot and see what happens? Because this market is not paying you to take that kind of risk. You can be down 30 percent in anything just because people feel like they want to sell. If I want to be more short, I will be more short in that name. If I have a long side, I have a $4 million position or a $3 million position. I don't have any shorts that are that big. I have a lot more concentrated risk on the long side than I do on the short side. I guess what I am saying is that I am going to be a little more careful on the long side. I think that is fine. I just diversify a little bit on the long side.

**K:**      You also look at the shorts as hedges.

**D:**      The shame here is that I have very good information on the short side. I just use them as a smart commodity and say, "Look, this is pretty good information. This could really blow up." My exposure is $8 to $9 million long, $11 million short, and $20 million gross. When I started, my exposure was $50 million gross. That was a mistake. I was out of rhythm with the psychology of the market. It's very hard.

**K:**      Why do you think it's hard?

**D:**      If you just want to be short, it's easy. I am not a guy who just always, every day comes in and wants to short a stock. I think there are going to be rallies in the market, and I don't have the P&L right now. If I were up, it would just be so much easier. I think I have said this a number of times. If you want to be short, okay. I am just going to stick with my viewpoint.

**K:**      You have a bias against shorts?

**D:**      I wouldn't say that I have a bias.

**K:**      You said a few minutes ago that you are net flat.

**D:**      I think over time that is right. Over time you make a lot more money on the long side than you do on the short side. I do think in certain periods you can make a lot of money on the short side, and the market is down now 20 percent in tech stocks. So, I am not up. I didn't capitalize on this 20 percent down thing. Now, if it goes up 10 percent, the last thing I want to do is lose another three million bucks because I was too short.

**K:**      So, you think it still might turn around, and that kind of long bias is influencing the way in which you are seeing the market?

**D:**     I didn't make money in this last 20 percent down thing. I usually make some money on the long side, and I reinvest it on the short side. It gives you the power to stick on the short side.

**K:**     Mastery is adapting your game to the changed circumstances. Why not take a greater risk by being short? It may make sense to look a little more at the short side than you are.

**D:**     I am just not that big on the short side.

**K:**     You are governed by your habits. The market is crowded. The information doesn't work. There is no follow-through. Why is this so difficult? What makes it so hard to trade shorts?

**D:**     For me, I just need to make my shorts when I have conviction about them as big as I have about my longs. I don't think that I need to be shorter.

**K:**     You have got to overcome the long bias. Psychologically, you think long is more risk-averse than short. I think because you are a little shell-shocked or a little anxious, you pull back and stop doing what is going to work the best under the current circumstances. When you start freezing a little bit, you get tense, and you don't do what instinctively works. You become more self-conscious.

**D:**     I think that's right. I am so afraid to lose money and look stupid. If the market goes up, you know your longs go up. That usually works.

The most stressful aspect of shorting is that the potential loss on the short sale of a stock is unlimited because theoretically the value could continue to rise forever. What makes matters even more complicated is that the stock's owner can demand the stock back at any time, and the trader has to return it—no matter where the price currently stands. So, in order to be a successful short seller, you have to be comfortable enough to act on your shorts despite this kind of stress and the knowledge that everyone around you is long. To become a master, you must face their own rationalizations about why they don't want to short.

## STRESS AND THE SHORT SQUEEZE

A short squeeze occurs when buyers force the price of a stock upward beyond the typical trading range. Those who have been shorting the stock begin to experience psychological pain that they will lose money when they have to buy the stock back (cover it). As the price moves up, the shorts are squeezed out of the stock. To cut their losses, short sellers are forced to buy it back at a higher price. At some point there may not be enough stock available to be bought back, and the short sellers are squeezed even more. At that point they are willing to pay whatever they have to in order to buy the stock back. This is known as a capitulation on the upside. Whether this leads to a full capitulation or not, it can be emotionally disturbing since the short seller is often psychologically traumatized by the short squeeze. So, learning to manage the stress of the short squeeze is crucial to becoming a successful short seller.

Traders often get carried away by their emotions on the short side. Sometimes they are unable to admit they are wrong early and become frozen, wishing for the stock to come down. The move itself generates strong emotions, and traders have to learn to hold their short positions when appropriate and cover their shorts to cut their losses when the stock is too strong or their original reasons for shorting are no longer correct.

Listen as one trader describes this kind of experience:

"I have a stock that went from 30 to zero. It was a bad business and bad people, and there were good checks and good work that I did the whole way. At one point it rallied from 16 to 20. It was a huge rally—25 percent. Then it went from 20 to zero. When it went from 16 to 20, I thought, 'Wow, this is painful.' But I had to stick with it. In the scheme of the 30 points, the four-point rally was not anything significant. So, I have also been trying to take the little bumps required to get the big trade right. I know this stock has problems. I know this company has a lot bigger problems than most people perceive. I look at the numbers, and they're horrible."

For most traders the emotional aspects of a short position can paralyze. They hold on when it is not working and hope that the next tick will be the highest and then the stock will start to fall. A master trader, however, watches the price of the short and isn't afraid to buy the stock back to keep losses down.

There is a psychological tendency to want to buy the bottom and short the top—that is, jump in on the long side at the actual lowest point of a stock and start selling short as the stock price hits the actual upside limit. That mentality can be troublesome to the short seller. You have to be skeptical but not cynical. You also have to be objective. If you are not objective, then you try too hard to get it right. From a money management viewpoint that can be deadly, because you may get stuck in far more speculative gambles than you can afford and may run the risk of blowing up.

You shouldn't short simply to short. You always must have a reason and create a thesis—a train of thought from which to trade. How well you handle a short squeeze depends on your ability to maintain your composure in the face of pain. The best traders can tolerate the price rises and get out when the price actions show that they are wrong. The master trader knows when to get out of the short by covering and taking a loss and can determine when to press the bet.

## STEPS OF A GOOD SHORT SELLER

While you will never completely reduce the stress of the short selling game, you can help minimize it by following the definition of a good short, developing a solid thesis, looking for missed earnings, and perfecting your timing and relevance.

### Defining a Good Short

There are several things to look for when selecting a good short—fraud, accounting problems, failed or weak management, shifting trends in the industry, reduced margins or profits, increased competition, or a company that is overvalued and likely to be sold off. Since there are also several types of shorts, each one requires an understanding of a different aspect of information. Some are based on understanding the structural weaknesses of the company. Others are based on the perception or understanding the false perceptions on the Street. Let's look at five different types of shorts:

1. *Macro shorts.* This is where a previously optimistic perception of a new technology has changed, or the economy has slowed and people are spending less.

2. *Micro shorts.* You short one company based on something specific about another company. For example, a retailer misses a quarter, and you short its largest supplier.

3. *Perception shorts.* Sometimes no matter how good the numbers are, the stock still drops. Although the perception of a weakening company may be wrong, it is still affecting the trading. The company's fundamentals might be solid, but expectations as reflected in the stock price have reached unsustainable levels; therefore, there is an opportunity to short.

4. *Fundamental shorts.* The company has a fundamental or structural weakness.

5. *Supply versus demand shorts.* Sometimes there are artificial imbalances among stocks. For example, you can short the new stocks being added to an index, because they are likely to go up artificially and temporarily on the day they are added to the index. At the same time you can go long on the index itself, which may initially drop at the time of the addition of the new stocks.

A short seller can also look for companies whose fundamentals are peaking. In such cases the stock prices have discounted all the positive fundamentals and aren't going to get any better. There is probably no positive news flow to come for these stocks, and usually that causes the longs to exit their positions.

In essence, short sellers try to identify issues facing a company or the industry as a whole that will make a stock go down. They look for fundamental flaws in the business and are attuned to negative news, innuendo, or other signs, be they subtle or concrete, which indicate that things aren't what they appear to be and that something could go wrong.

## Developing a Thesis

Short sellers incorporate many factors, such as macroeconomic data, company-specific information, and clearly defined events, to form an educated hypothesis about a stock's performance. Even though they may be trading on a short-term basis, they are still concerned about structural and industrial issues as well as sales and accounting numbers. They do not rely simply on price action or on general notions about the company but on highly specific details that are then subjected to a careful thought process. By focusing on specific dates, traders can provide themselves with a benchmark and a time frame in which to see if their conclusions are borne out or accepted by the market. They are on the lookout for any signs that their view will soon be embraced, since once their perception is no longer variant, the trading world will catch up and the stock will no longer be a good candidate for shorting. Serious traders also approach the market with multiple options so they can be prepared to get out of the position if the thought process or premise proves to be unclear or even wrong.

"Psychologically, you have to be able to ride out the discomfort when your hypothesis doesn't initially work out. The thesis provides a basis for differentiating between random and real market movement. The thesis helps you to notice when you are wrong. This isn't always easy," said one short seller.

"If you become too firm in your views and don't respect the volatility, you can be hurt," he continued. "You can't be locked into your game plan. You have to know which plans to follow as your expectations are or are not realized. For example, if there is a meeting and it doesn't go as you expected, then you have to reconsider your position. To do this, you need several scenarios and a thought process that is likely to change as both the price and information about a stock change."

## Missed Earnings

Another critical stock selection strategy is to consider missed earnings that underscore the fact that expectations may have been too high. When a company misses its publicly guided earnings estimates because, for example, it may have blown through its budget, the CEO may challenge the operating team to improve the next quarter. The team in turn may start scrambling to improve the bottom line and actually show temporary improvement without necessarily correcting the basic structural inefficiencies.

Missed earnings often trigger panic selling and lead to precipitous price drops and the withdrawal from the marketplace of buyers and sellers who have become price insensitive because the near-term outlook is no longer as favorable as originally expected. What's more, missed earnings in the most recent quarter or past two quarters might signal continued weakness in a company's targets.

In effect, looking for broken stocks with missed earnings and disappointed expectations is one way of selecting potentially profitable shorts. The strategy is to short them before the earnings reports. These stocks may drift up and then drop after reporting earnings. The key to shorting is to pick the time when the stock is about to roll over the crest of its upside and head downward.

## Perfecting Timing and Relevance

The master short seller not only seeks early access to information about a company, he also waits patiently until just before the information becomes known and relevant to the Street. Prior to that time, the data is theoretical. But eventually, for it to be of value to him as a trader, to give him a real edge, others must know it and act upon it as well. The master short seller is thus able to sense when his idea is becoming consensus and is skilled at figuring out when to start getting out of the trade.

The differentiated view must become apparent to the market. It has to reach the Street and change the way other traders perceive that particular stock. The information is relevant only if others eventually start selling a stock after he has shorted it.

Therefore, when assessing a short, the short seller needs to ask three important questions:

1. Is my assessment objective, not emotional?
2. What do I know that no one else knows?
3. When will the Street accept my differentiated view?

Although understanding the fundamental issues of a company is important, fundamentals alone are not enough to produce a successful short. Sometimes the best shorts are put on in anticipation of a change in perception. While the fundamentals may change very little, the anticipation of such a change in the fundamentals can drive a stock. In fact, the task of shorting is especially difficult in a bear market because the fundamentals count for less in this kind of market. The trader then must rely on other resources and remain flexible in order to succeed at it.

To be successful at selling short, you have to understand the timeliness of the available information. Making sure the information is critical and timely is more important for shorts than for longs because the market is naturally biased toward the upside. You have to determine when you think the information will affect the stock price, because others have yet to respond. As there are thousands of companies with questionable balance sheets and questionable practices, the market has to accept that information in order for it to be significant.

That is why it is important to contain your anxiety. You need to develop nerves of steel to keep from being too early. Often short sellers face adverse conditions or pain when making decisions on entries and exits. Trading successfully requires staying focused, disciplined, and unemotional in the face of great stress.

## Case Study: Short versus Long Methodologies

Dalton was one trader who was quite clear about the distinction between being long and being short a stock. When I met with him I asked him which game he felt was easier, the long-term game or the short-term game. Or were the two simply different?

**Dalton:** They're two different games. There are times when we are disciplined about it. We are short for the right reason. The stock will go down 15 to 20 percent for that reason, and we cover it. There are cases where we don't cover it, and the stock isn't really working, but it still helps offset some of the risk, and we will keep it on even though our fieldwork or the analysis suggests that maybe it's not going to go down 25 percent. I can affirm only three stocks in our portfolio that we should be short right now.

**Kiev:** Can you give me some background?

**D:** Consider this one particular business. It's an unbelievably expensive business and is never going to get strong enough to support where the stock is. There is a tremendous amount of competitive compressors facing it. It's a bad long-term business. But, having said that, it is a buzz-worthy name in tech.

**Kiev:** What role does buzz play in this?

**D:**   If one of the names among stocks with this buzz go up, they all go up. So basically you have to monitor 50 names. It's overvalued, and ultimately the business is going to plateau. By the time that happens, the stock could be 100 percent higher than where it is today. So, when you are short a stock like this, you actually have to think about all 50 stocks out there. If something good happens to one of those 50, your stock goes up. It's not a company-specific issue anymore, but a whole industry issue with too much risk. Something could happen that you don't expect. The odds are stacked against you.

**K:**   Can you give me another example?

**D:**   Sometimes there are just bad businesses. For example, this company we shorted had bad fundamentals, the cash flow was falling off, and there was regulatory risk. It's an energy company where things were falling apart. There was no second derivative. Nobody was going to say anything great that was going to help that business. I think that's the kind of short we should focus on. If it goes up we lose some money, but it's not the kind of stock that is going to go up 100 percent in two weeks. There are fundamental reasons why it's a bad business.

**K:**   Does your methodology work with both shorts and longs?

**D:**   Our long methodology is great.

**K:**   But would it apply to the short side?

**D:**   Not necessarily. It's not replicated on the short side.

**K:**   Because somehow or other you think the short game is a different game. But, for me, where I am coming from, the short game is the same game.

**D:**   I think that is fair. You touched on a good point.

**K:**   Does it take more effort on the short side than the long side?

**D:**   Absolutely, because there are the positive buys. If we are short a stock, we will probably lose a little bit of money in the immediate space. But long-term we will hopefully make money because there are accounting issues that no one has caught yet.

**K:**   It sounds as if you need to use the same methodology you use for longs. Some traders say, "We have never done well in our shorts." Well, that's fine, but if you have a strong methodology, you have a better chance of doing well. You need to have a really good story, really have a reason to short it. From my point of view, a successful trader will look at a short the same way he looks at his longs. He is looking for companies that really are going down. Then he tries to manage his risk in a sense by putting in stops. As the stock goes up it starts hurting him, but unless the story has changed he should hang in there with the conviction that it is going to go down. Then when it starts going his way, he should maximize his profit and not bail out the first chance he gets in order to avoid any more pain. The short side should be just as approachable as the long. Would it make sense to rely more on the fundamentals?

**D:** In my opinion, if a short thesis begins with the biggest bullet point or top bullet point, it's an expensive stock; that's not how I want to begin the search for shorts. Frankly, just like I don't think we look for cheap stocks on the long side, my personal opinion would be more opportunistic. You have to get a feel for what other people are feeling. We have had some shorts that are painful and expensive.

**K:** Is it fair to say that while the methodology being used to pick longs isn't really being used to pick shorts, it is the same research, the same process of digging in?

**D:** I think all of our shorts are well researched to the extent we are not taking the same exposure. We are not taking eight or nine positions on our best short ideas as opposed to our best long idea, which is 8 or 9 percent of the fund's capital. To a certain degree we do more research on the longs, but I think that's the nature of our fund where we have 10 to 15 core longs that we are running with. I have probably 40 to 60 shorts. There is no way to do the same amount of intense research on each short position.

**K:** What's the argument for having so many shorts?

**D:** I guess because we are comfortable enough. If you are comfortable enough, where you love an idea, it should be a substantial proportion of your portfolio.

**K:** Should the initial size be such that you factor in the amount you are willing to lose in comparison to what you think you may be able to gain? Can you set a figure so that you know when it reaches a certain point you must get out? The problem is that once you start experiencing pain, that messes with your psychology, and that's when stubbornness comes into play. But if you know (because you have determined it beforehand) that once it hits a certain number you are going to cut the position, doesn't that help you become more comfortable in the trade? Then, whenever you do lose, you know that you will never lose more than you planned.

Your thinking sounds very amateurish compared to how sophisticated your long strategy is. It sounds like you are looking for high beta tech stocks which will crash and burn and produce some home runs. That sounds a little amateurish. As savvy as you are on the long side, I would expect you to have a little more differentiated view of how to pick short stocks.

**D:**      I just think it comes down to being a little more opportunistic and a little more pragmatic. If we could outperform the market on the shorts, that would be tremendous.

**K:**      You have to import some of your strategy from the long side to the short side.

As you have heard, I am suggesting that Dalton think more deeply about his approach to shorts so that he develops his theses on shorts based on rational news in the same way that he chooses his longs. Once he removes his emotion and his anxiety from the process, he can make better decisions and size his short positions as coherently as he does his longs. However, some of the points he makes about shorts, such as looking at the entire sector as well as companies related to the one you plan to short, are logical and can contribute data that helps to reduce stress.

Shorting is another weapon in the trader's arsenal. It is especially relevant to those who want to run a balanced portfolio, capitalizing on the ups and downs in the market. But it is also a strategy that works best for those who are able to stay centered and trade in the zone. By identifying the elements of apprehension that muddy the waters in shorts, traders can craft a much stronger portfolio that is profitable regardless of how powerful the trends are in any one direction.

# CHAPTER 13

# Learning to Live with Stress

*D* *on was doing very well. He was moving toward a $5 million cushion and trading with great alacrity in a fast-moving market where most traders couldn't stay in one position too long. He was taking profits faster than he had ever done and was learning the short-term, catalyst-driven trading game. His performance was in great contrast to many of his old partners, who were down 13 percent for the year.*

*He meditated every day and was increasingly visualizing the trades he was going to make. He was using meditation to control his emotional responses and to avoid overattachment to his positions. In fact, Don was taking advantage of the stressful nature of the market when many of his peers were struggling.*

By becoming aware of the nature, emotions, and dangers of stress, you have taken the first steps toward overcoming its stranglehold on your trading career. The next step is learning not just how to manage stress, but how to use it to your advantage.

Most traders perform their duties by rote, according to what I call life principles. As I mentioned in Chapter 10, these are habitual ways of looking at the world, beliefs around which we organize our lives. These beliefs were ingrained in us when we were very young. As children, to protect ourselves against fear and the disapproval of our parents, we learned what behavior was acceptable and what was not. Thus, we developed a fixed set of response patterns that we carry with us into adulthood. These patterns invariably grow rigid and become defense mechanisms.

These automatic thoughts keep us from seeing the world, or reality, as it is. In fact, we are controlled by our automatic thinking. We see what is happening to us through a distorted lens. Our lives change, and our choices multiply once we are adults, but our life principles remain entrenched.

Happily, we can use the potent tool of self-reflection to stand apart from our life principles, to identify them, and to consciously change those that warp our interactions. By focusing a different lens on our past, we can reframe our perspectives.

This same theory holds with regard to the emotions you feel after experiencing a stressful trade. You see and experience events through the emotional reactivity of stress, frustration, anxiety, and tension. Because of this, you react with irritation and interpret everything as an imposition or as a source of your vulnerability and victimization.

But you can bypass these negative feelings by deliberately separating your emotions from your actions and reflecting on smarter ways to handle those emotions. The road to healing begins with observation.

## LEARNING TO OBSERVE

We are not an emotionless people, so we cannot rid ourselves of stress. Trying to resist, deny, or dissociate yourself from your emotions only increases the likelihood that they will grow in intensity. After a stressful trade, you need to permit yourself to experience the full range of natural emotions.

It is important to remember that there is a huge upside to looking dispassionately at those emotions and the physiological responses associated with them. You do not need to consciously or unconsciously keep them bottled up.

Unfortunately, some traders are embarrassed about their emotional responses and have found that others don't want to talk about them, either. It may be that you never learned to communicate your feelings, or you were encouraged to suppress them. You may actually believe there is something wrong with you when feelings bubble to the surface. This is particularly true with regard to all the bodily sensations associated with fear and stress.

Therefore, when dealing with stress, it is critical to learn how to open up, let your defenses down, and allow yourself to get in touch with the very feelings that you have the urge to suppress. The therapeutic task is to reactivate stressful feelings, experience them, and express them in order to defuse their power. The key is to fully articulate the negative feelings that continue to afflict you. In this way, you let go of the destructive aspects of these feelings and permit yourself to fully experience the stress as a neutral sensation. You learn from your mistakes and then leave the past behind.

All of this hinges on one critical exercise. *You must learn to distinguish between your feelings and who you are.* Your feelings or the thoughts associated with them are part of you, but they don't define your entire personality. Your feelings and thoughts arise naturally out of stress. You can stand back and experience them without reacting to them.

That's the first step in turning stress to your advantage.

I realize this sounds counterintuitive, but I have seen people make this separation many times, and individuals, however they feel about the idea of holding their feelings at arm's length and examining them, almost inevitably feel better once they try it.

For instance, I talked with one trader, Brad, about how his emotional reactivity to volatile market situations was negatively influencing his trades. Brad needed to apply in trading what he did so well on the tennis court. He needed to learn how not to allow emotional reactions to interfere with the game. In tennis, he uses relaxation exercises between points in order to clear his mind and concentrate on the point. We discussed how he could start doing something similar with his trading, and he decided to begin listening to meditation tapes with the hope that he could employ meditation techniques while he was trading.

You, too, can become familiar with your emotions rather than trying to maintain a stiff upper lip. Notice your reaction to your feelings, but don't do anything about it. Notice, too, your interpretation of the situation—and let it go. Don't make any impulsive decisions as a result of your reaction. Just allow your feelings to flow through you as a natural response to the events at hand and watch them dissipate like puffs of smoke or the clouds of vapor that materialize when you exhale in cold weather.

## Case Study in Visualization as a Tool to Diffuse Stress

In the following discussion, one trader describes how he plans to use visualization when faced with stressful events. In this way, he hopes to remain focused on what is critical and to ride out any accompanying emotional reactions. Here Preston compares his experiences with race car driving to his experiences as a trader. We discuss the benefits of visualization in controlling stressful reactions in both circumstances.

**Kiev:** What do you experience when you are in the zone?

**Preston:** There is a natural high. There is a definite satisfaction from it. I am trying to figure out how to get into it more often.

**K:** What do you mean when you say you're in the zone? Do you mean that everything is working for you, or is it a description of a feeling? Are you actually able to see things better?

**P:**          It's all those things. Time seems to stand still. I feel elated and totally in control. There is no anxiety at all.

**K:**          Is there a constant preparation?

**P:**          When I get in the zone, it's almost relaxing. But getting there requires preparation, hard work, and all those nitty-gritty things.

**K:**          Could it be that getting into the zone is a result of being totally focused?

**P:**          That's probably a big part of it. My wife thinks I go to the track because I like hanging out. But I tell her, when we go to the track we work hard. We work from seven in the morning until seven at night and then I go home, take a shower, and get on my computer to look at the data that we got out of the race car. I start going over things again until I fall asleep. It's an all-day affair.

**K:**          It's total absorption. So, are you doing more of that than you did in the past—with regard to your trading, that is?

**P:**          A lot more! I am really working at it. It requires some work to get into the zone.

**K:**          Once you get into the zone, do you have to raise the stakes?

**P:**          That's right. You have to make sure that it continues to be a challenge. That's why I am considering taking my racing to the next level. I am considering going pro so that I will have more competitive drivers to race against.

**K:**          So, when you talk about being in the zone, you are talking about the focus, the intensity, the way you are seeing things, the way you are dealing with problems. Extraneous matter does not distract you when you are in the zone.

**P:**          You are not cognizant of time. Unfortunately, trading is unlike other activities in that we don't have as much control over it. You know the market does dictate a little bit. When the market is dead, it's dead. You are not going to get in the zone. There is no zone. You're very relaxed when you're in the zone. I've had trouble with that part at times because I've gotten tense, and when I am tense I can't get in the zone.

**K:**          Do you mean that when the adrenaline gets going, it's hard to settle down?

**P:**          With racing again, what I notice is that I don't do as well when I get too tense. Now that I have some experience I hardly hold the steering wheel. I sit there and just consciously try to be relaxed instead of tensing up.

**K:**          You prepare. You focus. You build up for this event, and then you have to be able to ride the wave. You have to be able to

|      |      |
|------|------|
| | stay with it. But, if you are too relaxed you may not focus well enough, either. There is a balance. |
| **P:** | I agree. |
| **K:** | Okay, but let's talk about the other side. Sometimes stuff is clicking, and you are taking risk, and you are calling people. Things are happening and going your way. You are in the zone. Then all of a sudden the world isn't responding, and you start to slow down. That's when you hit a low. |
| **P:** | You can definitely have a low. |
| **K:** | So, you have to remember that you got to that point of being in the zone by preparation and by focus. You have to get back to work instead of letting the stress get you down. |
| **P:** | One time I got into the zone at a race on Sunday. On Monday everything was fine at work. Then I went to play tennis Monday evening, and I found I was still relaxed. I played my best hour of tennis. I don't know why. I just did. My strokes were perfect, and I found that I was still in that zone. Obviously driving has nothing to do with playing tennis. So, maybe it is more about a state of mind. |
| **K:** | Let's talk about how visualization can contribute to creating that state of mind. |
| **P:** | I use visualization with my racing. This past weekend I went to a new track. The whole thing about driving is that it's repetitive. You know the turns, and you have to do them perfectly. But when you go to a new track, you don't know the turns. So it's more of a struggle. By Saturday I was feeling frazzled. I was getting nervous, and I was trying too hard. So, I tried to remember my last race when I was in control. I asked myself what it felt like. I tried to put myself into that same winning mind-set. |
| **K:** | Visualize that winning race now. Tell me about it. |
| **P:** | I was just completely in control, completely in the zone, completely dominating. I remember what I felt like. I remember what I was looking at. |
| **K:** | Do you feel that way now? Imagine that you are actually there and reliving that moment. |
| **P:** | I am in the pit lane, and we are getting ready to go. I am putting on my helmet and my radio. Everybody else has gone out. People are coming up to me because they think that I am late or something is wrong, but in fact I am just waiting. Then I go out, and I am doing everything that I should be doing. I am warming up the car. I am warming up the tires. I am looking for my spots. I am coming up to pace kind of gradually, not all at once. The car feels better and better as the tires get warmer. |

**K:**        What are you feeling?

**P:**        It's calming, relaxing.

**K:**        Just keep doing it until you really feel like you are right there.

**P:**        I can feel it. It's calming. I take three deep breaths like I did the other day before the race.

**K:**        Are you beginning to understand that you have the capacity to reexperience that whole day, that whole event? You can get back into the zone without even going to the track.

**P:**        You're right! I feel it. I just did that half a lap. I remember what it looks like. I remember the view from my car. I see the track, and I see which way it goes. I see that there is a guy who is ahead of me who is in my class. I need to catch him. I am catching him. Everything is going fine. Now I am passing. I am calm and just letting the car drive itself. I am not muscling it. I am not going to go any faster if I squeeze the steering wheel. So relax and let it do its job. I feel it. I am calm and in control.

**K:**        You seem to say that race was a breakthrough for you. So, it can be an anchoring memory, something to which you can connect to help you get in the zone. It is no different from the actor who recalls a sad experience in his own life—say, the death of a loved one—in order to make himself cry at just the right moment on-screen. Now, let's apply this mind-set to trading.

**P:**        Okay.

**K:**        Can you recreate that sense of control with your trading experiences? You can't control the tires if they blow. You can't control the other drivers. But you can create a track for yourself in the midst of all the other tracks. Just like you found an anchoring experience in racing, you need to find a similarly powerful trading experience to help you achieve that same mind-set in trading.

Visualization helps Preston to get into the zone both at the track and now, in the trading room. In this centered state of mind he is better able to handle both the stress of car racing as well as the stress of trading. The more tuned into his experience he can get, the greater his chance of handling complex, high-stress situations and keeping his focus.

The same goes for all traders. The more they can get familiar with the physical sensations that come with their emotions, the more they can stand back and report on those experiences and overcome the inclination to make decisions in the moment of reactivity.

Anxiety and fear tend to be contagious and self-multiplying. When a trader can learn to observe these feelings and share them with others, he can discover that the feelings are harmless and will not escalate to a point where he loses his mind or loses control. Once he begins to ride out these experiences, he will also notice a diminution in the frequency of panic attacks and a gradual subsiding of the anxiety that occurs when he anticipates that fear is about to preoccupy him. He will experience a greater sense of being alive than was true previously.

You, too, can gradually discover that your emotions are a normal response to stressful events as well as to events that are given a frightening symbolic significance. As you become comfortable with the associated symptoms of anxiety, you will be less likely to create excessive anxiety or to overreact to anticipated events. To the extent that you can learn to do this, you can ride through many events that normally you would avoid. Gradually you will find that situations that triggered anxiety no longer do, and you will be able to engage in more anxiety-producing situations, exposing yourself to greater risks.

## Observation Exercise

Here is an exercise to help you observe and learn from your emotions:

1. Recall a specific trade that has caused you an unusual amount of stress.

2. Remember the specific emotions you felt as a result of your stress: anger, frustration, fear, guilt, anxiety, aggression, grief, and so on.

3. In your journal, write down all the facts of the situation, including how you felt and what you would like to change.

4. Now write down the typical emotional reactions and bodily sensations you experienced in relation to the situation.

5. Write down what the situation meant to you. What was your interpretation of it? What did you think would happen? For example, did your heart start palpitating? Did you think you were having a heart attack? Or were you angry with your friend for giving you bad advice or your risk manager for convincing you to get out too early? Did you want to hit someone or scream?

6. Is your perspective of the situation a longstanding one? Does it express a point of view about the world that you developed long before the current event? (For example: "I have no control over my life." "Everything always turns out bad." "I have to look like I'm in control.") How much does this fixed, historically based perspective or life principle color the facts? Ask yourself what the actual facts are, and make a list of them.

7. Now, imagine and write down an alternative, new interpretation of the situation, based on the facts you have listed.

## CREATING NEW LIFE PRINCIPLES

Some traders recognize that they are blocking their emotions and begin to seek emotional outlets and opportunities to express their distress. They recognize the negative impact of the emotional blockage and are willing to struggle through the impasse to improve their trading. They can then break through the emotional numbing that has kept them from being fully engaged in their careers.

However, for many individuals, it is hard to slough off life principles. Regardless of how outmoded the life principles are, they are as familiar and comfortable as old shoes. The problem with old shoes, though, is that they have holes and no longer really support well. It's the same with life principles. While a trader may be reluctant to let go of his typical way of handling things, the longer he stays trapped in the past, the longer he will be a victim of his circumstances.

Everyone can change his or her responses. Whenever a trader starts to become agitated, frightened, or even angry, he can stand back, analyze the sequence of events, and put a new interpretation on his feelings so that he can allow the tension and anxiety to pass and can begin to see the possibility in the situation. Finally, he can learn to ride out his emotions until they pass. He can change his perspective.

When he can create a new way of experiencing the world, he will no longer be automatically bound by his old reactions. When he begins to focus on the actions he can take rather than focusing on maintaining certain feelings, he frees himself from the past and can experience a wide variety of emotions without being dominated by them. By differentiating the event from the emotional and physiological responses or personal narration or interpretation, a trader can begin to notice that the event is neutral and has occurred independently of himself.

Many traders are surprised to discover that once they are able to tap their emotional reserves and convey their stress, they are also able to relate to and learn from their past experiences. They have less need to cover up their feelings and a greater capacity to be fully present to their trading experiences.

In this way, traders make it possible to hurdle the barriers that keep them from being fully intimate and connected to their lives. Remember, all of the emotions that traders have are normal responses to stress. While it is also normal to want to hide these feelings or to be embarrassed by them, it is far better to face emotions, recognize them, ride them out, and even share them.

## REFRAMING NEGATIVE THOUGHTS

What is the value in learning to ride out negative thoughts and emotions? It's a method of being truthful with yourself and of separating your thoughts from the rest of your being. Once you make that distinction, you will see those negative thoughts as interpretations, as pieces of the numerous thoughts that go through your mind. In that process of watching your own thought patterns, you have an opportunity to see your intrusive, nightmarish thoughts (and the emotions associated with them) shrink.

When you experience anxious thoughts, it is possible to identify them and choose how you are going to react to them. Self-monitoring is again a key element here. If you recognize these thoughts and choose to function in terms of a more positive set of expectations, you can ride out the discomfort and function beyond the limits set by these anxious thoughts. It is possible to change your level of anxiety by changing your thoughts.

For example, I met with Galvin on a Wednesday. He was concerned about "being in a slump" and afraid of being wrong. As such, he was trading very cautiously and trying to get out of positions too early because he was worried about making even more mistakes. I suggested that he discuss his recommendations with me before he traded them so as to be able to recognize and discount his emotional reactivity and make more proactive calls.

The conversation we had relieved him of much distress and gave him a perspective about letting go of the negative framework of "being in a slump." He was able to start finding positive things in his work process. By Thursday he was beginning to see that he had some opportunities and was optimistic about moving forward.

A clue to your distressing thoughts can be found in your vocabulary—in the phrases that you consistently use, sometimes even unconsciously. The words and statements *what if*, *I can't*, *I'll try*, and *but* have been shown to keep alive negative symptoms. Words such as *impossible, if only, however, difficult, ought to, should*, and *doubt* often reflect underlying principles of fear, trepidation, and limitation. Pay attention to how frequently you use these negative words so that you can begin to replace negative concepts with words of possibility and commitment.

When you eliminate ideas of limitation like "I'll try" or "I can't" from your response system and substitute positive assertions such as "I will do this by next Tuesday," you will define a new way of trading—a positive, assertive, self-defining way that will allow you to bypass the symptoms that have previously governed you.

Consciously changing the automatic words from negative, fearful concepts to positive images begins to change the way in which you perceive the world. An old saw that speaks to this is: "Fake it until you make it." You might not totally believe your positive phrases at the outset, but all that counts is operating as if you did believe them. It is not so much that the world changes, but you begin to tune in to new dimensions in the world.

First, identify some of the beliefs that dominate your thinking and that distort your perceptions of events. What do you think about yourself and others as a result of your life principles? You may, for example, believe that:

- You can't trust anyone.
- The world is an unsafe place.
- You cannot enter into an uncontrolled situation.
- You must do everything on your own.
- You are damaged goods.
- You have been irreparably harmed.
- No one understands what happened to you.
- No one else ever experienced the kinds of stressful events you have.
- There is no possibility of recovery.

If you operate from such thoughts, there is no chance that you can become the master of your fate. These thoughts set you up to be a victim and limit your opportunity to be free of the past. If you consciously or unconsciously accept these principles, you are likely to place responsibility for your trades on forces or people outside yourself, further reducing your ability to become the pilot of your own destiny. This sets in motion a self-fulfilling prophecy of helplessness and terror.

Reframing allows you to respond to anxiety-producing experiences in a positive way. Focus on the positive vision of things whenever you are inclined to see things in the negative light. Begin to experience the world through a new set of empowering principles such as making a difference, being responsible for your trades, choosing what you have, forgiving others for what they have done to you, and letting go of resentments.

Whenever you notice that you are thinking in old, repetitive patterns, project your focus onto the future. This requires an attitude of greater self-awareness than you might be used to, and it means you have to monitor your thoughts carefully. When you do this, the events before you will be shaped by your future objective. Your thoughts will shift from negative responses and begin to take on fresh meaning.

Let me make this clear: A positive set of objectives does *not* eliminate the negative thoughts or emotions that appear as a result of stress, irrespective of whether you reach your goals. The key to commitment is to recognize that negative thoughts are transient and to get yourself back on track—even in the face of self-doubt and uncertainty.

There is vast literature on the use of positive thoughts to eradicate negative thoughts. My view is that you define a larger framework for your life with space for both positive and negative thoughts. You don't need to try too hard to suppress the negative thoughts, since this will only intensify them. A better approach is to notice these thoughts and gradually shift to the positive thoughts. Slowly increase your capacity to stay focused, recognizing that the negative is likely to recur even in the context of the positive or fulfilling activities.

Anxiety is part of the human condition. It's perfectly human to have those bodily reactions. It's human to have those recurring thoughts. Again, if you can allow yourself to ride out distress and can utilize the techniques like relaxation exercises and journal writing, every thought, every emotion, becomes merely information to examine, not a definition of who you are.

When you can free yourself from the past, you can begin to trade in terms of what you are able to do. You can recognize that your trades provide an opportunity to play out an unwritten script. You are no longer tied to notions about yourself from childhood or from the stress that have been boxing you in.

## Self-Assessment Test

Try to answer each of these questions honestly, in your mind. Then, in your journal, write down an example from your life that illustrates each answer.

- What can you lose if you let go of your victim mentality, if you give up the avoidance pattern and your ritualistic approach to so many elements of your trading?

- How much do you avoid responsibility, and how often do you avoid taking risks, preferring to stay on familiar terrain?

- To what extent have you handed over the controls to others?

- To what extent do you let others make decisions and take false responsibility for your endeavors?

- How much does this pattern keep alive the unpleasant feelings of insecurity and insufficiency?

- How much does this excessive dependence impose on other people's lives?

- How resentful are you of their control over your trades?

- How much chronic conflict, frustration, and rage are perpetuated by the symbolic reaction you have established?

## CHOOSING AN OBJECTIVE

One of the most powerful and effective ways to master the symptoms of stress is to choose an objective and then start trading in terms of that objective. The sense of control and mastery that you will gain from this is enormous. You begin to trade and manage your portfolio in terms of what you choose rather than reactively in response to events. You begin to focus attention on the steps critical for reaching your objective rather than continuing to function in terms of your fearful responses.

By focusing on the reason for undertaking a task, you can then become absorbed by your purpose rather than by the anxiety and the reactivation of fearful feelings. If you can change your focus to a larger objective or vision, it becomes possible to move forward more effectively with less anxiety. Here concentration, step-by-step planning, and taking action become critical ingredients of the goal-oriented focus and help to dispel the anticipation of fear.

When you create an objective and work toward it, you change the way in which you experience the world. Having an objective allows you to become absorbed in the moment in front of you and encourages you to concentrate on the steps you can take rather than becoming involved with your own mental preoccupations and concerns.

A first step is to begin to take risks in the face of uncertainty. A good analogy is learning the sport of rock climbing. One of the maneuvers that seems to be the most risky is rappelling—swinging from a rope over a cliff or rock face. The best rock-climbing schools teach you this on the very first day, not from a huge cliff but over a short drop. As a novice, you may be quite hesitant as you step backward toward the edge, playing out the rope buckled to a harness around your waist. With the next step, you leave the ledge and step into nothing but space. In that instant, most novice climbers feel a rush of exhilaration, even if they are just 10 feet off the ground. They suddenly feel like they are flying—yet they are hitched into a harness and securely held by the rope. From that moment it becomes easy to lower yourself to the ground from higher and higher ledges.

How willing are you to let go of the familiar and begin to do what you haven't done before or to do what seems scary? Take on new projects and new behaviors, and you will begin to discover new things about yourself. You can allow projects and future objectives to govern your choice of actions rather than being chained to the past. You can develop an entirely new set of habits when you are willing to face the unknown. By making small changes in your everyday routines, you will see how much you are locked into familiar and comfortable ways of behaving that may actually restrict your growth as a trader.

## DEFINING NEW PRIORITIES

A second step is to change your priorities. Your concept of how things ought to be has prevented you from trying new ways of being. The power to change stems, in part, from being prepared to break free of the demands of the past, the "shoulds" and the "musts." Allow yourself to encounter the discomfort associated with not doing what you think you should do. This gives you the room to expand in other directions.

Currently, you are being governed by a set of expectations established in response to certain stresses or events. Your task now is to discard these expectations and to function independently in terms of the objectives you have consciously chosen.

There is a well-known experiment in which ulcers were induced in monkeys by depriving them of the capacity to make choices or to control the events in a cage. This experiment is relevant to your ability to choose what happens to you. Choosing circumstances and handicaps, even those over which you have no control, is critical to the process of change in terms of reducing any sense of helplessness that you may have.

To overcome the residual effects of powerlessness that are so much a part of stress, you must take charge of your life. You may not be able to change your circumstances, the events that trigger stress, or even your emotions, but you do have the power to choose how you react to all of these. When you reframe your response to the events of your life and to your symptoms, you will begin to see how you control what happens to you and how you face each trade.

For example, Howard was taking advantage of the panic in the market. He was buying up a lot of AAA-rated bonds that had fallen with the market but which afforded him great opportunities. He had a real feel for the markets and had developed a knack for viewing what was going on from a game theory perspective and taking advantage of unrealistic divergences in the market based on fear and emotion. In other words, he used the feelings of the crowd to help interpret market sentiment and make a prediction as to what would happen next. He used his own emotions and the emotions of others to his advantage.

You, too, can change your perspective. When you do this, you will be able to find meaning and purpose in what initially may appear senseless and meaningless. When you shift your viewpoint, you can see the challenge in adversity.

Your trading career is not preordained. The choice is yours. You can define a new purpose to govern your trades. You can see stressful events as challenges designed to strengthen you for the future. Indeed, you can seize the moment and look for a more fruitful use of your energy.

If you are interested in pursuing the themes explored in this book, contact me at www.arikiev.com.

# CHAPTER 14

# Exercises and Practical Applications

*D* ouglas was up about $5 million on $100 million of capital over nine months and hoped to be able to make $15 million the following year. His strategy was to find five good $3 million trades and about 10 to 15 $1 million to $2 million trades. Given his expectation that some things wouldn't work, he figured this would help him achieve his $15 million goal.

*In order to do this, he was trying to get bigger in high-conviction ideas, hold them longer, and not take his profits so impulsively. To help him make these adjustments, I suggested he keep a list of trading rules based on his assessments of his trading performance. By reviewing this list, he could monitor his performance. He also kept charts of his trades so that he could periodically review when he was getting in and out and could learn to stretch his time horizons in terms of how the market moved and how he responded. At the time he was having difficulty in momentum-driven markets but hoped to correct this.*

Mastery is the capacity to function fully in the world with the resources available to you. It means that you no longer bemoan your fate; instead, you change it. But change requires more than an intellectual effort. You cannot simply process information about how to change. You must put yourself in an unfamiliar situation and do something that is quite unexpected or that you don't ordinarily do. To achieve a true makeover of your habits, you must engage in real experiences. Only real experiences, as uncomfortable as they can become, have the power to transform your trades.

As a result of the stress and fear that you have experienced in your trading, you might have begun to retreat from the game or at least might have lowered your expectations. Perhaps you have decided to withdraw, to not engage fully. You may feel pessimistic about the possibility of recovering or restoring your trading or even maintaining the status quo, let alone ever reaching higher goals.

But don't give up. The power to change is immediately accessible to you. And I promise you this: It is absolutely worth all the effort you must summon from within yourself.

Coping with the stress of trading starts with a vision. Set a goal and then decide what steps are needed to reach that objective. Take action toward that objective, even if you can't stop yourself from noticing all the internal obstacles or points of resistance that get in the way.

You will come across constant opportunities for creativity and motivation if you allow each situation to impact you with all its originality and uniqueness. Living fully in the moment enables you to live beyond your self-protective ego and beyond just thoughts of survival. Although you might feel some trepidation, facing this realm of reality will help you to discover amazing resources and support in the world around you.

Your stress won't completely disappear. But you will function better by creating a new set of concepts and by acting in the present consistent with your vision, overriding your stress. Once you distinguish between the facts and your body's responses to emotional thoughts, you begin to deal effectively with a whole variety of stressful situations. Once you reframe your trading in a large enough context, you can identify difficult situations as really being stepping-stones for enormous growth.

Again, change *won't* occur by simply reading this book. You must initiate action toward a specific outcome. This takes time because you will be visualizing a new concept of your trading game and implementing new measures to realize your vision. In particular, it takes time to overcome notions of yourself embedded in your unconscious and to begin to align your life with your new perspective. But having decided on your larger objective, even seemingly small acts can guide you along the path to your goal.

What's important is what you do daily, in real time, to make change happen. There is only the present in which to live. So if you think that you already *are* okay, you are already poised at the starting gate. There is only a vision of the future, which, like a lens or a pair of glasses, provides a perspective from which to access the present.

You undoubtedly have heard these lines: "How do you get to Carnegie Hall? Practice, practice, practice." "What does it take to save $100? A hundred dollar bills, a thousand dimes, or 10 thousand pennies." In other words, your question for yourself daily should be: "What can I accomplish *today* toward my objective?" Let your commitment define your action, rather than doing things in the same old defensive way.

When you're really committed, you are likely to be uncomfortable, uncertain, continually looking for what more you can do. This is what test pilots call pushing the envelope. You will always be challenging yourself, and stretching, literally or figuratively, brings on momentary aches. Nevertheless, despite momentary stressful feelings, you will discover extraordinary things about your capacity as a human being. This is not about trying to change a Chevrolet into a Cadillac. It's about how to take the Chevrolet from 10 miles per hour up to 50—how to become more of what you are capable of becoming.

Ultimately, to truly improve your trading and manage your stress, you must step into the void of uncertainty. This requires that you take one step at a time having thoroughly armed yourself with the best information you have gathered to point you toward good decisions in trading. Action is the key.

Let's look at some practical applications of how to handle the stress that you will encounter on a daily basis.

## THE MOST BASIC STRESS BUSTERS

Our minds and bodies have limited resources, and traders, like all humans, can handle only so much. Some of the best means of preventing stress from taking you out of the game are some of the most simple, but often neglected, items on our "to do" list.

### Exercise Regularly

Exercise provides a physical outlet for that pent-up stress you encounter during the trading day. It is especially beneficial if you can visit the gym on your lunch break, but many traders enjoy after-work or weekend activities. Biking, boxing, and running serve to promote not only physical wellness but psychological stability as well. If you find it difficult to establish some sort of organized exercise routine, consider the benefits of even short, moderate bursts of exercise. Most traders can at least take a brisk walk around the block (or up and down a few flights of stairs) once during the workday.

### Eating Right

We all know that eating right is important for our heart and general health, but you might be surprised to learn that eating right is also related to how you handle stress. When you eat a heavy, fatty meal, you are more likely to feel sluggish and not up to par. If you eat too little, your body has a harder time concentrating on the task at hand, and your mind is likely to wander when your stomach grumbles. Eating healthy, well-balanced meals and staying well hydrated will help give you the mental and physical energy to fight stress all day long.

### Getting Enough Rest

While our society seems to be proud of workaholics, a solid night's sleep and moments of relaxation during your waking hours are necessities. Your body was created with a need to regenerate. When you push yourself too hard for too long, there will be consequences. In addition to getting enough sleep on a nightly basis and taking breaks during the workday, it is also important to take periodic vacations so that you can recuperate and freshen your perspective.

* * *

In addition to these three, there is another basic stress buster that is important to always keep in mind: *Trading is not your life*. Don't be afraid to have hobbies and outside interests. Develop deep and meaningful relationships. When you do this, even when the worst trading situation becomes a reality you will discover that your life is not over.

### Meditation, Visualization, and Mental Rehearsal

A well-thought-out plan is of little value to the trader who cannot put it into action. Yet many traders who devise wonderful strategies have trouble executing them. Meditation, visualization, and mental rehearsal may help you learn how to cope with stress in a more productive way. By mentally recording various scenarios in your head, you can learn to replay difficult situations, practicing how to best deal with the stress.

By practicing these types of exercises, you can learn to address issues in a more peaceful and relaxed manner and to face difficult days with the confidence that you can handle anything that comes your way.

## WHAT TO DO WHEN YOU HAVE A BREAKDOWN

A breakdown occurs when you come face-to-face with obstacles that prevent the unhindered flow of action. However, it is not what people often call a *nervous* breakdown—a lay term usually referring to any kind of

## A Simple Breathing Exercise

1. Sit in a quiet spot by yourself. (Alternatively, attend a meditation session at your gym or yoga class.) Focus on your breathing. Keep the word *smoothness* in mind. Let your breathing and body become smooth.

2. Notice the smoothness of your breaths as you breathe. Feel your body letting go and becoming calmer.

3. Now let your mouth open a little, and when you feel ready, let a sound form as you exhale. Make whatever sound emerges with the least effort, as you continue to focus your attention on the smoothness of your breathing and your body.

4. Don't try to make the sound. Just let the sound flow out of you easily. If there are others in the room doing the exercise, note how soothing their sounds are. As you let the sound flow, your smoothness will expand to include the others in the room, and their smoothness will include you.

5. Gradually all of you will come together in one smooth sound or chant. Pause for breath and pause whenever you begin to tense up.

6. The sound or chant may change from time to time, rise and fall in volume, and change in pitch.

psychological collapse, which could be anything from a mild stress response to a serious psychosis. The kind of breakdown I am talking about here is a failure in communication, a faltering in the effort of moving toward your goal. A breakdown connotes a withdrawal of energy, a loss of focus. When your progress is stopped by your inhibitions, fears, or past perspectives—for example when, like Dustin in Chapter 6, you are paralyzed by indecision—you are having this kind of breakdown.

## Breakdowns and Breakthroughs

You cannot have a breakthrough—that moment when you step beyond certainty and, armed with the very best information you can gather, you make a large, confident, but perhaps controversial trade based on a high-conviction idea—without a breakdown. A breakdown points the way to areas of possibility. But there is, naturally, an intense urge to deny the reality of a breakdown. It's more comfortable to rationalize away your problems so that you don't have to face them. It's human nature to shy away from a breakdown or a setback.

Each time you stumble, you can use that moment to your advantage. It is the moment when you have come face-to-face with your own inclination to backslide or to downplay what you're doing because you don't want to

## Image Awareness Exercise

1. Sit firmly in your seat with your feet planted on the floor. Close your eyes or stare at the floor or wall.

2. Imagine that you are a tree stump in the mountains. Visualize yourself and your surroundings.

3. Try to describe yourself. What kind of stump are you? What's your shape? What kind of bark and roots do you have?

4. Get into the experience. How do you feel as a tree stump? What kinds of things happen to you? For example: "As a stump, I am old and twisted. I am sawed off, leveled. Chipmunks sit on me and crack nuts."

5. Near the tree stump is a cabin. Become this cabin and get into the feeling of the experience. What are you like? What's inside and what happens to you?

6. Near the cabin there's a stream. Become this stream. What kind of existence do you have? How do you feel as a stream? What kinds of experiences do you have as a stream?

7. While you are the stream, talk to the cabin. What do you say to the cabin?

8. Imagine the cabin answers back. You have a dialogue; what does the cabin answer back? Become the cabin and talk to the stream.

9. Now say good-bye to the mountains, the cabin, the stream, and the tree stump, and come back to your current room and existence.

10. Think about your experience of being the stump, the cabin, and the stream. Do it in the first person, present tense—"I am." Your last comment should be relevant to the now: "As a trader, I am ..."

run the risk of not succeeding. This is the moment to ask yourself questions like these:

- How reluctant am I to let go of the past in order to let life be as good as it can be?
- How hesitant am I to accept my intrinsic power?
- How much am I holding on to the negative past as opposed to recognizing the glorious future that's available to me?

A breakdown is a challenge. It exposes what you are lacking in your personal arsenal or what more needs to be done to produce specific results. To learn from your breakdowns, you need to ask yourself:

## Simple Visualization Exercise

You can use this visualization exercise in almost any situation where you feel the need to center and calm yourself. It is a metaphor for a safe zone. Once you get the gist of the exercise, it is almost like carrying around a gold nugget. Whenever you are feeling nervous about a new situation or upset by an intrusive memory, you can reach into your pocket, metaphorically hold the nugget, close your eyes or stare at the wall, and bring your mind back to a state of relaxation.

1. Breathe slowly, evenly, neither forcing nor holding back the natural flow of air. Your body knows how to breathe in a regular, easy fashion, and the only trick to relaxed breathing is to listen to your body's own messages.

2. Once you have relaxed and regulated your breathing, focus on some pleasant place you have visited or imagined. It could be a lovely beach, or a peaceful meadow, or a quiet room in a house.

3. Imagine you are there, in this special place. Take in all its sights, smells, sounds, and feelings.

4. Stay here, in this place, for as long as you can.

While this exercise will not necessarily diminish the stressful feelings that you are likely to encounter, it can help you learn how to cope with them in a more productive way.

- What would I do differently if I could do it over again? What could I have done that could have avoided the breakdown?
- What was missing from my actions?
- What can I learn from the breakdown that I can put into place in order to produce the outcome I want?

Consider what might happen if you looked at every breakdown as the start of a breakthrough, at every adversity as the seed of possibility, at every calamity as transient and temporary. In other words, rather than seeing complications, you can begin to interpret events through a new light that allows you to see problems and crises as challenges and adversity as opportunity. When you do this, you are effectively restructuring your cognitive map of the world. You are setting the stage for creating possibility and breakthrough.

The key to moving from a breakdown to a breakthrough is to act now. Don't procrastinate until you are certain of the outcome. The result is less

**Journal Writing Exercise**

1. Consider a problem or a breakdown you are currently dealing with—whether it involves recurring stresses, significant losses, relationship issues, or other difficulties.

2. Write down all the elements of the problem that seem troublesome.

3. Now, try to differentiate between the facts and the interpretations of the facts. What are the facts, and how much of what is problematic is your interpretation of the situation? Consider how much of what you see is really an interpretation based on a long-standing life principle rather than the actual facts of the situation.

4. Realize that you can change the circumstances or your perspective of the circumstances by creating a new interpretation or principle from which to lead your life. Using the same facts, write a new interpretation.

5. Can you see any possibility in dealing with the situation from the viewpoint of the new interpretation? If you do, write about this new way of handling it.

6. Do you see how the situation might improve if you can relinquish the old interpretation and substitute your new one? If so, write about what that improvement looks like.

critical than the process—what you do in the here and now. Your life can begin in the next moment. Each day offers the opportunity to create a new challenge or larger framework so as to move into that next moment. The issue is to keep taking steps to express your potential and become who you are capable of becoming. When you can see situations as they are and can face reality—that things are the way they are and that they don't have the meaning you attribute to them—you will be able to create your life in a more powerful way.

## Previous Triumphs and Pertinent Truths

To become a seasoned and successful trader, you have to develop extensive experience and to hone your trading skills. While disappointment is natural, you can minimize it by noting it and then striding past it. Another way to move beyond a major failure is to recall and concentrate on triumphs that you have experienced in the past. You may even want to make a list so that you can review them after big losses. By consciously making an effort to remember good outcomes, you are counteracting a natural tendency to recall past failures.

Another thing you need to do is recognize any truth that may be behind your feelings. Do you really lack certain skills? It is wise to address this question. If the answer is no, then recognize that your feelings are just a result of the current situation. But if the answer is yes, then begin taking the necessary steps to learn the skills that you need.

Another consideration when facing a disappointment is to remember to think in terms of the big picture. One trade will not make or break any trader. When you put pressure on yourself to succeed immediately, you are setting yourself up for more stress. By considering your long-term progress, you are taking a more relaxed and realistic view of success.

There will always be factors that you cannot control. So, concentrate on those that you can control. Take into consideration your overall win/loss ratio, your risk/reward ratio, how well you planned and executed your trades, and whether or not you are following your trading strategy. Winning traders trade consistently and profitably. They think realistically and positively.

## Taking a Break

Traders who are experiencing a breakdown must also consider the possibility that they need to take a break from their daily routine for a while. While many traders balk at this suggestion, it is important not to be afraid to allow yourself a brief vacation, especially if your strategy seems to have quit working. Taking a few days off or going on a short trip allows you the opportunity to step back and reevaluate. Take some time away from trading for psychological recovery. Attempting to work through a slump or continuing to trade when you are not mentally or physically feeling well only increases the likelihood of mistakes. Our moods color the way in which we see the world. And if we aren't seeing the markets or our information in an accurate and honest way, then our trades will reflect that misinterpretation.

No strategy will work indefinitely. If something seems wrong, then stop and look at the details. Consider the problem and see what needs tweaking to get back in the game. Take a look at the markets. What has changed? After making some adjustments, test your new theories on smaller trades instead of jumping headfirst back into the game with large amounts of capital. Remember you have to survive to trade another day.

Breakdowns should not be the end of the game. They are inevitable. Winning traders know how use their setbacks as motivators to do better next time. Keep a positive attitude. Examine mistakes, but don't obsess over them. Adjust as necessary. Make corrections when needed, but don't give up entirely. Identify what went wrong and change it. By keeping an upbeat approach, you can grow into an experienced and wiser trader.

## Finding the Right Motivation

Part of combating missteps includes finding the proper motivation to persevere even in the face of difficulties. Most traders might imagine that big wins (i.e., money) should be the primary motivation for continuing to trade. But that isn't necessarily so. Winning traders don't really concentrate on winning. They concentrate on the *process* of winning. This is more than just a play on words. Thoughts of monetary gain can quickly become frustrating when winning seems elusive. Therefore, it is better to find a more productive means to motivate yourself.

Some traders gain motivation from the thrill of trading itself or from looking at a trade as one big puzzle that needs to be solved. Others are motivated by the idea of trying to decipher what the markets are going to do or what move others are going to make. Many traders put a competitive spin on the game. The point is to find an impetus outside of money; the best motivator will be one that keeps you excited, energized, and in the game.

While monetary rewards are enjoyable, successful traders keep a healthy attitude toward money. Your wins define the framework of action that you need to take, but paradoxically the greater the amount of money, the more you must renounce your focus on it. Set your goal, and let it determine your strategy and sizing of positions, but then stop thinking about it. This takes some practice and effort.

### Conducting a Self-Evaluation

A large part of managing stress is performing self-evaluations. By asking yourself a variety of questions and assessing the answers in an unbiased way, you can make productive assessments of both your specific trading plan and your psychological makeup. By making necessary adjustments, you prepare yourself to deal more effectively with the inevitable stress. So, consider carefully the following list of suggestions and questions. Take note of areas in which you need work.

- Are you developing high-conviction ideas based on fundamental, analytical work (such as visiting companies and building models)?

- Are you sizing your high-conviction ideas commensurate with your profit target and deployment of capital in a risk-managed way? You have to learn when to get big by factoring in market conditions, trends, 200-day moving averages, and other technicals as well as knowing the risk/reward profile of a trade. If you have high conviction and a 2:1 risk/reward ratio and there is an 85 percent chance of being right, you can size the position fully.

- How important is it for you to have a catalyst or an event that is going to move the price of a stock?

- Do you discuss your mistakes with other traders so as to get an objective opinion and learn how to improve your performance?

- Do you recognize when the markets are driven by macro factors and sentiment (as opposed to fundamentals)? When things are becoming risky, do you shrink your portfolio and take the gross down?

- How many good ideas can you expect to have in the period of one month? It shouldn't be unreasonable to expect three or four. Have you considered how you are going to create great ideas? Where are you going to get them?

- What kinds of screens can you run? How much more work can you do to improve your edge so that you can take advantage of knowing something that others don't yet know and can get into trades before they become crowded?

- When making a trade, do you have a process to manage slippage (i.e., to handle the loss of the value of a stock secondary to transaction costs)? Do you have high-quality ideas?

- Do you understand that sometimes it is better to reduce your amount of trading, to have fewer positions and hold them longer?

After reviewing some of the preceding questions, you may want to address the following questions to specifically outline your personal plan of action:

- How would you assess your P&L generation year-to-date (YTD) (excellent, satisfactory, needs improvement)? Why?

- How would you assess your ideas generation YTD (excellent, satisfactory, needs improvement)? Why? In your answer please address consistency (or hit ratio), frequency, and position sizing.

- What is your P&L target for next year? How do you plan on getting there?

- What are your goals (non-P&L-related) for next year?

- What are your longer-term goals? What is important to you in terms of career development, responsibility, and longer-term vision?

Remember, failure is nothing more than not making the effort. So, how you approach the process of stress management is important. Be willing to keep going in the face of discomfort. Don't define yourself by your feelings or your automatic thoughts. Notice that you can take action independently of what you are feeling or thinking. You will still feel the physical pains and the psychological emotions of stress, but you can make those initial forays despite those sensations. Soon, you will observe that you can begin to overcome doubts, sidestep emotional reactivity, and function in terms of what you have committed yourself to do.

## IMPORTANCE OF COMMITMENT

Let me reiterate what I said earlier in this chapter: Commitment is critical. Commitment requires that you design a structure of support to ensure you will do what you say you will do. The structure is an action plan related to the objective. It enables you to keep asking for support, to keep telling the truth about what you want, and to keep admitting to breakdowns so that you can do what is necessary to reestablish contact with reality. The more you can banish your ties to the past and can break free of negative emotions, the more you can find new purpose in your life.

One way to do this is to keep a running checklist of the problematic events in your life and your trading on a daily basis. Track your reactions to new events so that you can begin to gain objectivity about your automatic responses and decisions in moments of hesitation. In this way you should be able to link your defenses to the events in question. The insight you produce will give you greater self-control so that you can relate to events not through the filter of your past experiences but with a realism you might never have known before.

When you approach tasks in this way, you recognize how much preparation is part of the action. You don't rush headlong into the action to produce the result. You take your time. You are analytical and emotionally neutral.

Apply what you learn to the next situation. Give 100 percent of yourself to your action. Do what you can in the present moment, and then move on and do all you can in the next moment. Don't dwell on what might have been or on the opinions of others. Focus on being totally present in the next moment.

Your task is to stay focused in the face of the inclination to overreact, to overcontrol, and to try to force the result. You need confidence and faith in the outcome and an awareness that all you need to do is keep taking one step at a time.

Work with life as it is without paying attention to notions of either failure or success. It is important to shake off the fear that something may not succeed and approach decisions with an optimistic outlook. Believe that things will work out when you finally reach a certain objective.

Operate from a perspective of sufficiency, and you can see the beauty in the moment before you.

You cannot get rid of all the stress in trading. Even if you could, it would probably change the game to such an extent that you would no longer enjoy it. But you can learn to live with and actually use those stressful emotions to your benefit. Start by becoming an observer of your own thinking. Then devote yourself to your vision. Promise the results, and trade in a manner that is consistent with that promise. Make decisions based on what step should come next in the process of aiming toward your goal. Embrace the anxiety as part and parcel of the trading game. Expect it. Notice it. But don't let it affect your decision-making abilities. When you fail, get up and try again.

In order to trade successfully, you must act with stress as a constant, like the prevailing wind currents. If you wait for a stress-free trading environment, you will never trade. While it may be uncomfortable at times, commit to doing what you know you need to do—no matter how you feel at the moment.

Review the ideas in this book regularly. Put into practice the exercises you have learned in these chapters. Practice them until you get better at handling anxiety and controlling your response to anxiety. And remember that both losses and wins can yield stress. Reaching your goal is not going to eliminate stress any more than any other exercise this book has outlined will. Therefore you shouldn't concentrate so much on the goal itself as on the process of reaching the goal. Ultimately, mastery is about tapping your potential.

If you have any experiences that you'd like to share, I'd be happy to hear from you. Please contact me at www.arikiev.com.

# Index

Printed and bound by CPI Group (UK) Ltd, Croydon, CR0 4YY

16/04/2025

14658516-0001